Teach
and
Reach

for Classroom Miracles!

Lessons on Teaching With Love

Teach and Reach

for Classroom Miracles!

Lessons on Teaching With Love

Wendy Byard

FaithWalk Publishing
an imprint of CSS Publishing
Lima, Ohio

TEACH AND REACH FOR CLASSROOM MIRACLES!

FIRST EDITION
Copyright © 2008 by
Wendy Byard

Published by FaithWalk Publishing, an imprint of CSS Publishing Company, Inc., Lima, Ohio 45804.

Scripture quotations are from the New Revised Standard Version of the Bible, copyright 1989 by the Division of Christian Education of the National Council of the Churches of Christ in the USA. Used by permission.

14   13   12   11   10   09   7   6   5   4   3   2   1

Library of Congress Cataloging-in-Publication Data

Byard, Wendy,
     Teach and reach for classroom miracles! : lessons on teaching with love / Wendy Byard. — 1st ed.
        p. cm.
     ISBN-13: 978-0-7880-2615-7 (perfect bound : alk. paper)
     ISBN-10: 0-7880-2615-1 (perfect bound : alk. paper)
     1. Teaching—Religious aspects—Christianity. 2. Love—Religious aspects—Christianity. I. Title.
     LB1027.2.B93 2008
     371.102—dc22

                                                                    2008049189

Names and descriptions have been changed throughout this book to preserve the privacy of individuals.

ISBN-13: 978-0-7880-2615-7
ISBN-10: 0-7880-2615-1   PRINTED IN USA

For Dorothy Kitchen Crites —

a wife and mother,
a devoted church organist,
a lover of learning with three college degrees,
a deaf person who taught the handicapped and imprisoned,
a survivor of the Depression,
a world traveler to the birthplace of Jesus,
a gentle caretaker of neighborhood cats and backyard goldfish,
a quiet gardener,
a deep woman,
a believer,

my cherished grandmother,
my smiling ally —
who revealed to me, more than any other, the love of God on earth.

If I speak in the tongues of mortals ... but do not have love, I am a noisy gong....

— 1 Corinthians 13:1

Endorsements

After reading professor Byard's work I was impressed by her passion and the depth of her thinking in taking Christ's commandment to his followers to reach out to all with agape love as a part of her vocation. I could not put it down. The book with its many pertinent personal examples and deeply felt conviction shows how the efforts of any single Christian to seriously and deeply share the love of Christ can reach people in ways that could never be imagined. It is not simply a work for the teaching profession but reminds us all that in our own vocations we are all ministers and all teachers of agape love if we would simply take time to listen to the children of God the Lord puts in our lives, and to react to their needs by simply loving them as we love ourselves. It is a must read for all who call themselves people of Christ.

Reverend Todd D. Smith
First Presbyterian Church
Lapeer, Michigan

*The best way to leave a lasting legacy is to touch the lives of those to whom we are closest. One of the greatest historical relationships where this life-giving reality has the opportunity to take shape is when a teacher influences the life of his or her student. Wendy Byard applies a lifetime of experience as a daughter, mother, wife, and teacher to articulate in a powerful manner the keys to developing relationships. She also reveals how to create an atmosphere of love that gives every child the opportunity to reach his or her full potential. In **Teach And Reach For Classroom Miracles!** Wendy unlocks the code that will guide you into a world where "miracles take place in students' lives, which then reverberate throughout the world." Her personal Christian testimony is an inspiration, which shapes her practical recommendations that can be utilized by anyone. A must read for leaders and especially teachers!*

Greg Kelley
Executive Director
World Mission

*Professor Byard's book, **Teach And Reach For Classroom Miracles!** is a straightforward account of her own journey to live a life of Christianity and to carry this through in her teaching. This book will compel teachers to question how they teach and inspire them to approach their calling from a higher level. Her thoughtful account of her own self-doubts and efforts to make her vocation of teaching a reflection of her life in Christ gives practical ideas that are not overwhelming but easily accomplished. In this age of ever-increasing academic demands in the classroom, this book will compel teachers who read it to stop focusing only on curriculum and start teaching their students with love.*

Shirley A. Harris, PsyD
School Psychologist

Table Of Contents

Author's First-Day-Of-Class Letter To Her Students

Dear Students:

Welcome! I'm so excited you are here! For many of you, this is your first semester in college. It may even be your first class. Others may have more experience. Regardless, I know how it feels to be in a new situation. I was a student once myself. I also have collected hundreds of student letters over the years like the one below that reveals fears many of you may have:

> *My name is Chris. I have been out of school for thirty years! I am scared to death about being back in school, but it is something I have wanted to do for many years. Time, however, was always against me. Now I am re-tired from a job I hated! So I look forward with some hesitation to living up to the potential I know I have, starting with this one class to see how I do. I may seem calm, cool, and collected, but inside I'm a mess. I want to succeed!*

I'm here to tell you what I told Chris: Relax, smile, and have faith! You are about to have a fun, challenging, and maybe even transforming fifteen weeks! I also want you to know where I'm coming from as a teacher. You could call it my mission statement. Now be prepared, some of you may find it a bit corny or even shocking, but I'm willing to risk your initial reaction. Here goes:

"In this classroom, I will teach you with love."

I know. Love is a strong word. We don't hear it often in a public setting. So, what do I mean? Simply put, I will strive to teach each of you with the following qualities:

- patience
- kindness
- generosity

11

- humility
- courtesy
- unselfishness
- good humor
- honesty
- sincerity

It's a tall order, but I believe every one of you is worth it! So put away your concerns and anxieties. Instead, let's have a positive and purposeful experience together learning information, developing skills, creating meaningful thoughts, and communicating them most effectively. Much good is about to occur! Just read Chris' words at the end of the semester:

> *I can't thank you enough for helping me realize my potential for writing! You made my start in college easy and fun. I will always remember your kindness!*

So here's to an outstanding fifteen weeks in which we all learn much from each other in the *best possible way.*

Wendy

Introduction:
The Miracle Of Bill

The classroom was silent as I faced the dusty chalkboard and began writing the night's lesson. Suddenly, I heard a rustling noise. I quickly turned, and that's when I saw him — a most unusual student. The man was older, thirty perhaps, large, even bear-like, with a wandering eye and a pronounced limp.

"May I help you?" I asked hesitantly.

Often, on the first day of class, community college students end up in the wrong room. This older man, with his somewhat off-putting, even unnerving appearance surely was not in my beginning English course. However, his answer surprised me and, I'm ashamed to admit, slightly dismayed me.

"I'm here for English 099."

My class.

Within minutes, this force of nature was overwhelming me with the details of his life: years of drug abuse, a debilitating car accident, and serious doubts about attending college. For the next 45 minutes, Bill held me captive.

"Oh boy," I thought, "it's going to be a long semester."

That night I left the college feeling slightly anxious about Bill's presence in my class (and life) for the next fifteen weeks. The next few classes confirmed my fears: Bill was a challenge. First, there were the noises. Bill liked to sigh. A lot. Deeply and loudly. He also liked to clear his throat quite often. Other students would sometimes roll their eyes or shift irritably in their seats. Then there were the impulsive, loudly blurted exclamations during quiet times. Bill would yell, "I don't know how to do this!" "What does this mean?" or "How am I supposed to figure this out?"

He would become easily frustrated, even angry, by material and activities that challenged him. As the days turned into weeks, it became increasingly clear to me that Bill was afraid. He did not want to fail. He had faced so many past disappointments and obstacles. I began to truly recognize the depth of his worries.

I also began to truly care about his success.

However, devoting myself to Bill's cause wasn't always easy, and it certainly wasn't always fun. Bill could drive me nuts sometimes with his many questions and challenges. But I made a firm commitment to him. We met before class, we talked during class, and we continued discussions after class. Oftentimes we would sit at a table in the commons and chitchat about Bill's life. In the computer lab, we vigorously discussed his assignments, while we contemplated his past events and future dreams. For Bill, I always had a bright smile, a kind word, and a pat on the back. In all our everyday conversations and interactions, I consistently made an effort to show Bill my commitment to him. I even prayed on his behalf.

And guess what? This challenging older student who began with little confidence but much heartache showed up to my class every single night; he never missed one. Week after week, Bill tried his best, consistently demonstrating a strong willingness to learn and improve. And that's just what he did.

Surprising even himself, Bill passed my class.

Then one night at the semester's end, I finally quizzed Bill about something that had long been on my mind.

Feeling a bit frazzled that evening, I asked, "Bill, why are you always so early to my class? Fifteen minutes seems reasonable, even twenty. But you are always here some 45 minutes before my class begins."

In my mind, I also was thinking a bit selfishly that it would be nice to get a small break from Bill occasionally in order to write my lesson on the chalkboard in quiet. So, I continued: "I just don't understand why every class period you need to be here this early."

His slowly delivered reply caught me off guard. Pushing worn glasses up the bridge of his nose, Bill looked at me intently and said, "This is one of the few places someone cares about me and praises me. I like it here. I feel good."

His words touched me deeply.

As I drove home that crisp fall night, I was full of elation — happy for Bill and happy for myself. I had been given the privilege and joy of witnessing and taking part in Bill's journey and success. That night, as I looked out over the darkened roadway, I vowed that I would strive to not only devote myself to every student, but

I would *love every student*! Yes, love! I would do my best to love and actively express it to every child of God I was privileged to teach. Once again I realized that it was me who also was the student. Bill was a gift who taught me a most valuable lesson, a lesson about God's love.

Through the years I've been teaching, I've been blessed with many such "gifts" and witnessed many such success stories, or as I think of them, everyday miracles. I've seen students find confidence, courage, hope, determination, belief, understanding, and love for themselves and others. Some might not look at these transformations as miraculous. But I choose to agree with Albert Einstein. He claimed that "there are only two ways to live your life. One is as though nothing is a miracle. The other is as though everything is a miracle."

So, what exactly allowed for Bill's triumph in my English 099 course? What exactly creates such everyday classroom miracles?

In *Teach And Reach For Classroom Miracles!* I share "My Journey To Love," the path I took as a teacher, wife, and mother that ultimately led me to my belief. It is the number one lesson I've learned. Love — the profound *agape* love proclaimed by the Bible and exemplified by the life of Jesus Christ — is the key to teaching. God loves us deeply and unconditionally, and when we truly believe in him and allow the Holy Spirit into our hearts, God's love will move in us to create classroom miracles.

This belief will surely find disagreement. Many people might argue that it is enough for a teacher to be capable, motivated, and yes, caring in the classroom. That is what is required: knowledge, skills, and possibly affection. Some might claim that it is inappropriate to love students; we should reserve love for spouses, children, and other family members. Still others might believe that love for students is not even possible. I understand these lines of thinking. I thought the same things once.

But now I wonder, *Is skill enough? Is affection enough or is something more required? Something more powerful? Something more transforming? Something godly?* One of my students once wrote to me, "I truly felt that you cared more than you were required ... I believe characteristics like yours are what make good

15

instructors great." Yes, it was a nice compliment, but it was her use of the word *required* that really got me thinking. When it comes to teaching, just how much caring is required? What is enough? How do we know? Where can the answer be found?

The Bible, of course.

The apostle Paul tells us that in every arena of life, love is the key. Love is everything. Love trumps everything.

> *If I speak in the tongues of mortals and of angels, but do not have love, I am a noisy gong or a clanging cymbal. And if I have prophetic powers, and understand all mysteries and all knowledge, and if I have all faith, so as to remove mountains, but do not have love, I am nothing. If I give away all my possessions, and if I hand over my body so that I may boast, but do not have love, I gain nothing.*
>
> *Love is patient; love is kind; love is not envious or boastful or arrogant or rude. It does not insist on its own way; it is not irritable or resentful; it does not rejoice in wrongdoing, but rejoices in the truth. It bears all things, believes all things, hopes all things, endures all things.* — 1 Corinthians 13:1-7

How many teachers, and those who have great influence in others' lives, though qualified, caring, and certainly skilled, are simply resounding gongs or clanging cymbals? How many of them are patient, kind, generous, humble, courteous, and unselfish, among the other qualities of love revealed by Paul? How many of them *delight* in their students as God delights in us? In other words, are they *loving* those they are charged to teach? If not, can they truly help cultivate miracles?

The Bible also contains this thought-provoking quote: "God hath set some in the church, first apostles, secondarily prophets, *thirdly teachers*, after that miracles." Why is it that God put teachers third in the line of important people he set in his church? It seems the Bible is telling us that teachers only follow apostles and prophets in importance! They are given even more emphasis than miracles! Did you know this? Did you realize that God places such value on teachers? I didn't. But this passage made me wonder: "Why is that teachers are seemingly more important in God's plans than miracles?" French writer Francois Mauriac said, "To love someone is to see a miracle invisible to others."

Perhaps God put teachers before miracles because, with God's love and vision, he wants teachers to strive to emulate Christ's loving example. Teaching with love would allow for the creation of miracles in others' lives, ultimately creating a godly, loving world. God, it seems, infuses teachers with great influence in order to carry out his will to create everyday miracles in the lives of his people.

Therefore, in Section One of *Teach And Reach For Classroom Miracles!* I make the argument as to why love must lie within the hearts and minds of teachers and other mentors. People do have the capacity to create God's world of love. When teachers are their most loving, they can help others fulfill their highest potential, creating miracles in people's lives that reverberate throughout the world.

Ralph Waldo Emerson wisely observed that "the power of love, as the basis of a state, has never been tried." Yet, what stops teachers, who influence millions, from making love the basis of their syllabi, their lesson plans, their classrooms, thereby helping to make God's love the basis of people's lives?

In Section Two, I draw on my own experiences in order to provide concrete ways teachers and others can make love the basis of their teaching and actively express it. My minister recently called it "emotion becoming motion." I also heard it referred to as laboring on love. In this book, love is a verb; it must be expressed. What good are loving feelings without action? The Bible tells us more is required: "... Let us love, not in word or speech, but in truth and action" (1 John 3:18). So, in this section I provide teachers with specific ideas and methods that I use in my classroom — loving actions that flow from the Holy Spirit through me and out to my students.

Although my beliefs and ideas might seem to apply only to teachers, my lessons on love can be applied to anyone in a mentoring position. Whether we educate as professors, high school or elementary teachers, youth leaders, coaches, or kindergarten aides, we are all teachers and can choose to respond to God's call. However, be prepared: The Bible expects much from teachers. "Not many of you should become teachers, my brothers and sisters, for you know that we who teach will be judged with greater strictness" (James 3:1).

So, I ask you: "What are you doing and why?" Yes, you may be teaching with diligence, skill, and commitment, and of course that is admirable. But do you truly delight in your students as God delights in you? Are you undertaking your mission with God's love, the quality of all human existence the apostle Paul called the "greatest"? Do you love your students? Are you using that greatest, most powerful force to help create everyday miracles? Willa Cather, the twentieth-century novelist, said, "Where there is great love there are always miracles."

I am often reminded of the miracle of Bill. I still see him around campus from time to time. He smiles broadly at me as he shares his continued success story. Bill is now taking more college classes and seems to be confident and succeeding — miracles. I believe the love I imparted, God's love, definitely played its part in Bill's ongoing, miraculous journey. Author Barbara de Angelis said, "Love and kindness ... always make a difference."

Do you have a Bill in your life? In your future? If so, are you embracing God's love and letting it flow to him and to every child of God placed in your path? Are you striving to create everyday miracles? *Teach And Reach For Classroom Miracles!* will not only open your eyes to the opportunity for miraculous possibilities, but, through the Holy Spirit, it will help you create them. Isn't it time you began your journey to love?

Section One:

My Journey To Love

The Day I Almost Gave Birth In A Four-Door

I slowly drove down the two-lane country road, nervously glancing out the rainy window; I could feel my amniotic fluid leaking. It was a horrifying feeling. I was almost thirty and seemed ready to deliver my first baby any second, perhaps in my car all alone. Despite the fact that I was about to give birth in an aging Skylark, you still might assume this day would rank as the highlight of my life. However, to echo Charles Dickens, this day, though certainly a best of times, also would rank as one of my worst.

I was a high school teacher, and as any teacher knows, some days the kids are rough. I had recently returned from a trip to Hawaii (while over eight months pregnant!). There I was, back in the classroom, supposedly impressing my young students with my self-centered stories of glimmering beaches and late-night luaus. "We sipped fruity cocktails out of pineapples. I had so much fun!" Yet, I was happy to be back teaching in my small Michigan farming community and looking forward to delivering my first baby in the blossoming spring. Everything seemed great.

The day ended uneventfully. After the last school bus roared out of sight, I returned to my quiet room and began the daily task of grading papers. About 2:45 p.m. the seemingly centuries-old intercom crackled to life.

"Wendy, could you come down to the counselor's office? She has something she needs to discuss."

Trepidation seized me. You didn't get "called down" unless there was a disgruntled parent or annoyed principal. I walked down the now-silent hallway, wondering what I did wrong. I turned the corner, and under the fluorescent lights I saw the petite yet commanding counselor, who firmly motioned for me to sit down.

"We have a situation, Wendy. A few of the girls in your fourth hour class have been circulating a nasty letter. Basically, it's a list of all the things they don't like about you. They passed it around, getting other students to sign it."

I felt like I had been punched in the gut. She handed me the wrinkled paper, and my eyes darted over their adolescent scrawling.

"Wendy is always talking about her trip to Hawaii." "Wendy always goes to the bathroom but never lets us go." And there were even more painful and personal comments like, "Wendy's skirt looks awful on her huge stomach."

There were thirty comments — all that tore me down in petty ways and seemed to express a dislike of me. I was devastated. I walked back stiffly to my classroom, quietly shut the door, and began to cry. I was devastated. I wanted to be liked so badly — to be loved. I thought I had done everything right to earn my students' respect, if not affection. I cried long and hard for myself.

Then, exhausted, I crept out of the school. Not only was I heartbroken, I was ashamed. As a first-year teacher, I had such high hopes for myself. I felt like a failure. Maybe I really didn't belong in the classroom. What was I thinking? Me, at thirty, starting a new career. Clearly, I must not be very good at it. The kids hate me. Negative thoughts pounded my brain as I made the 25-minute drive home, sobbing once again the entire way.

Suddenly, my stomach began cramping, and my water broke. I frantically drove to the local ball fields where my husband was practicing for an upcoming softball game. But I couldn't see him, and, being that I was ready to become a mother any minute, I could hardly leave my car. So there I slumped, the motor running and the windows fogging up, feeling more pathetic and ashamed than I could ever remember. Why, on what should be the best day of my life, did I have this awful experience? Why, on this of all days, did I have to feel so ashamed and unloved?

Fortunately, everything turned out fine with the birth of my daughter. Within the hour my husband had called me, found me upset, and rushed us to the hospital. That night my daughter, Haley, was born. She was perfect.

Yet, in the back of my mind lurked that mean letter. It was like a boulder pressing on my heart. Even as I held my beautiful newborn daughter, my mind darkened and obsessed on my students' hurtful words. Over and over, I questioned: "Why did these girls do it? Why didn't they like me? What was wrong with me? And why, of all days, did this happen *today?*"

I didn't realize it at the time, but that event would begin a change in me. It was one of those pivotal moments in life, and it led me to begin questioning my foundations — who I was and why, what I believed, and how, as a result, I treated others. I think it's more than coincidence that this transfiguring experience took place on the day I gave birth because, looking back, it seems it was a rebirth for me. That fateful day started me on a journey that has since taught me many lessons about life, but most importantly, lessons about God's love for me and for others.

—

My Early Years As A Resounding Gong

Let me set the scene. It was springtime in Michigan, a great time of renewal in my cold, long-suffering state, and suddenly cheery daffodils and bold tulips were bursting forth all over. It was a sunny April day, still cold, but everyone was joyous. Out my front window, I jealously watched happy neighbors jog by, their children, like prisoners suddenly released, racing ahead on shiny bicycles.

Yet what was I doing? How was I enjoying this wonderful time of rebirth? Well, instead of teaching ninth-grade English or soaking up the newly arrived sun, I was dealing with the sudden and dramatic change of first-time motherhood. Instead of waking up rested and donning a fashionable, neatly pressed outfit for work, I was dragging around the house day after day in the same yellow stirrup pants and spit-stained floral tunic. It seemed like my child bawled constantly. Thus I spent my days (and nights) either laughing somewhat hysterically or crying and begging my precious child to learn the difference between night and day. (No, 1 a.m. is not bedtime.)

I was exhausted. I was disheveled. Sometimes I felt really miserable. In fact, at one point during this supposedly perfect time in a woman's life I cracked a broom against the garage floor while screaming at my husband. (My poor husband. He really was a trouper.)

Now don't get me wrong. I know I'm painting a disturbing picture; however, it's a time I know many women have endured. We all love our babies and feel blessed. My little girl is beautiful, simply perfect. But I was in a fragile state of mind brought on by little sleep, new responsibilities, the pain of surgery, and the realization that I was mostly alone in this new task. My husband had returned to work, and the caring, helpful people in my life had quit stopping by. No more UPS drivers dropping off pink floral arrangements. Now it was just me.

Added to this mix were the negative thoughts and feelings still banging around my brain due to that intercepted classroom letter. My students' words had cut me deeply, and I couldn't help obsessing over them. Night after night, while I rocked my baby in the quiet morning hours, I continued to wonder why my students reacted to me the way they did. After my daughter's birth there had been no time to question my students, to get answers, and thus I had no closure. The wound remained open and raw, and the exhausting questions continued.

It was a strange time for me — a period of my life in which I felt great happiness, but I also experienced real pain. There were moments of great joy, but inside of me, often hidden, there were times of deep sadness and uncertainty.

Soon the days became weeks and, since my union contract specified an exact eight-week maternity leave for a C-section, I had to return to my classroom with only a few days left in the school year. Of course, I was anxious. All I could think about was that last day when it seemed so clear many of my students disliked me or at least were not connected to me in any real way. I really did not want to go back to my classroom, but I did.

Thankfully, the first day back was uneventful. It was a blur as I acclimated myself to the high school world. Then, on my second day back, a humid June afternoon, I was grading papers at my desk when the two "editors" of the nasty note rushed into my classroom, straight up to my desk. I was immediately anxious.

"Mrs. Byard, Mrs. Byard!"

My spine stiffened. *What now?* I thought. *Haven't you hurt me enough?*

"Mrs. Byard! Brittany wants to run for class secretary, but Ashley already got all our friends to sign her petition! Wasn't that mean! What are we going do? Please, please help us!"

Well, this was rich. Two months ago these girls wounded my spirit with their terribly hurtful letter, and now they were coming to me for advice! I was stunned. Yet, as they stood before me, and I looked closely into their sad, youthful faces and imploring eyes, I began to see them more clearly: These were simply children in young women's bodies. They were still growing, maturing, and learning. In that moment, I was able to put aside my personal feelings and talk to the girls, giving them advice on how to deal with this latest adolescent crisis. After they had gone, smiling and thanking me as they left my room, I had to laugh (sort of). Weeks earlier they had me in tears, sobbing in fact, yet now I was their buddy, their confidante, in just another teenage drama. To them, their mean letter about me was completely forgotten.

I learned several lessons that day. One, if I was going to remain a teacher, especially a high school teacher, I needed a much thicker skin. Teenagers can cause a lot of grief knowingly or unknowingly. Two, I needed to forgive them. I, too, had needed forgiveness throughout the years. Somehow, I had forgotten my many mistakes while I focused on their transgression. The experience also taught me that children, while often loving, can be immature and fickle. That is the nature of youth. One minute a teenager hates you — a minute later she wants to be tucked in with a kiss.

Did the realization of their capricious nature make me feel better? A little. Kids will be kids, right? However, I was still wounded by their earlier words as I was not entirely convinced that their words and deeds were purely the result of being youthful. In my heart, I felt there was more to the story. I put on my teacher's game face and acted as if all was fine, but inwardly I still felt pain and longed to know: Why did that event happen? What initiated that response in them? Why did they react to me that way?

At the time, I didn't realize I was beginning a journey that would lead to many personal changes. The first step on this trip involved me as a teacher. I began reflecting earnestly on what kind of teacher I was and why. Many people back then would wonder why I needed to reflect or change. I was friendly and enthusiastic. People liked me. Over lunch once, my mother compared me to a glass of champagne — always cheerful and bubbly. I also tried hard. I put a great deal of effort into creating quality lesson plans that I thought my students would not only learn from but enjoy.

How could this effervescent, dedicated teacher draw such an ugly response from her students? You would think that such a happy personality would be loved. In reality, it was mostly a shallow relationship. Back then, I cared much more about myself than I did my students.

I can still picture myself in front of the classroom, day after day, serving myself in some way.

"Oh, I can't wait to have my baby. I'm so excited; you know it's my first child. Has anyone ever been to Hawaii? I'm so excited about this trip! I wonder what kind of food I'll get to eat? Probably lots of pineapples. And I can't wait to see a volcano!"

Blah, blah, blah.

As I replayed those tapes in my mind, I sadly realized that much of my interaction with my students was about me. I was the center of the show. I also assumed that by simply being nice and cheerful, I was connecting with my students. But niceness and cheerfulness don't build relationships, and they are poor substitutes for sincere love. Most importantly, what I learned that day, and the lost opportunities can still hurt, is that *I did not love my students.*

Right now you're probably thinking to yourselves, *What?! Love?! What does she mean, love her students?*

Well, I mean several things. First, I was insincere. I played the part of a friendly, interested teacher, but in reality, I was most concerned about myself. I didn't truly care about the students — their needs, their concerns, their joys. I didn't strive to develop one-on-one relationships and make deep connections. In other words, I wasn't really there to serve *them.* I was there to serve myself, the syllabus, the principal, and the school board.

Like many teachers, I thought it was enough to simply like my students, to feel random flashes of affection now and then, and to rest easy in the self-contented belief that my hard work and the quality of my lesson plans was, in the end, all that is really expected of a teacher and all that really matters. Why would I serve them? Love them? Teachers aren't expected to love students, right? Who has heard of that? In fact, that is one thing teachers in training will not read in their textbooks or hear in their professors' lectures: "Love your students."

So, I loved myself.

At the time, I didn't know better.

Fortunately, a new day was coming.

Throughout this period of new motherhood and early career, I probably did more reflecting about myself than I had ever done. Becoming a mother and teacher, with the ensuing experiences and feelings, pushed me to begin contemplating a great many things. Strangely, I began thinking a lot about God. I say strangely because I was not a churchgoer. Growing up, I rarely went to church and had never been educated much about God or any religion. I knew little about the Bible, and as I grew older I told myself (and others) God was make believe.

However, very slowly a thought began to grow big in me that maybe God had been trying to communicate with me for a long time, but I wouldn't listen. For many years I had felt a spiritual pull, a seemingly small, gentle voice speaking to me, calling me. Yet I constantly told it to "shush," or I ignored it. I wasn't sure why I was experiencing this need to explore God, so I pushed the urge away. As I got older, I was having more fun concentrating my newfound intellectual capabilities on the game of trying to derail others from their spiritual beliefs.

"There is no God!" I would claim with superiority to my classmates. "He doesn't exist. All you have is yourself. Man is alone in this world."

Oh yes, I was smart. I had taken the college philosophy classes and just enough other courses in order to feel smug in that adolescent way that parrots the thinking of others without having to do any real critical thinking for yourself. On the day my daughter was born, that afternoon when I sat in my car and cried, that moment I felt so absolutely lacking in control and confidence, self-worth, and love, my assuredness in a great many things began to crumble. I was humbled and vulnerable. In that state when I felt lacking and unloved, it seems I began to finally hear a voice other than my own: God's.

Some people can recount a particular moment or day when they were jolted awake and reborn. Perhaps they were sitting in church on Easter, heard a particular Bible passage, and a golden light shone through stained-glass windows. I'm not saying that's what happened to me, that I became instantly aware of God's love and embrace that day in my Skylark. However, I do believe something changed profoundly that day and in the weeks and months to follow. In fact, I believe God gave me that day as a gift, a best and worst of days, the day my beautiful daughter was born and the day I felt somewhat crucified, to jolt me awake. It shook me into awareness. It opened my eyes.

That was many years ago, and since then I have given birth to two more daughters. When my girls were little, I went back to Michigan State University to earn a master's degree. I wanted to be able to stay at home with them and teach occasionally. I left high school teaching to become an English instructor at a local community college. It was during this time of change and questioning that my husband and I began attending church. As I said, it was a force, the Holy Spirit I know now, that was pulling at me. We soon joined the local Presbyterian church, and I began hearing Bible passages that encouraged my contemplation and new belief in God and his love for me. These are a few passages that called to me:

> *[God] who saved us and called us with a holy calling, not according to our works but according to his own purpose and grace. This grace was given to us in Christ Jesus before the ages began.* — 2 Timothy 1:9

> *In this love, not that we loved God but that he loved us and sent his Son to be the atoning sacrifice for our sins. So we have known and believe the love that God has for us. God is love, and those who abide in love abide in God, and God abides in them. We love because he first loved us.* — 1 John 4:10, 16, 19

> *The Lord opens the eyes of the blind.* — Psalm 146:8

Finally, I believed.
There was a God, and he loved me.
Like many excited new Christians, I became active, hoping to serve God and others. I enthusiastically taught Sunday school and

vacation Bible school. I joined the deacons, even becoming the moderator. I also committed myself to a little sister in the United Way Big Sister/Little Sister program. Then there were the countless hours as a mother, wife, and teacher that taught me many lessons, as well as the many church sermons that continued to transform my mind and heart.

It was a rich and busy time. I was learning about God's love, and his Holy Spirit was helping me to grow in countless ways. I now realize that these many lessons and experiences were serving to change me — to give my life a godly direction and deepen me as a person.

When I look back over these events of my life, the day my daughter was born will always stand out and be remembered with incredible joy, an amazing day, but it will also be remembered as a day I suffered with considerable mental anguish. I've since learned that painful, pivotal events challenge us and teach us, forcing us to grow and make decisions, to be, as many say, reborn. Yes, that fateful day started me on my Christian journey. But what of my journey as a teacher?

They say when you break a leg, the break heals so thoroughly that the bone is actually stronger than the original tissue. I still carried around a sense of brokenness, an unease that I wasn't meant to be a teacher. What would I do with my brokenness and my pain caused by those students' unloving words? Would I become angry and bitter? Would I blame my students? Would I distance myself from them, lose my confidence, and leave teaching? Or would I heal and become stronger, finding a new direction, a new vision, and a deepening that comes only from opening myself to God's love and his plan for me? When I thought about it, I realized that the teacher I was, the person I was, lacked a truly loving spirit, the Holy Spirit. I was like the dry bones in Ezekiel's vision.

> *The hand of the Lord came upon me, and he brought me out by the spirit of the Lord and set me down in the middle of a valley; it was full of bones. He led me all around them; there were very many lying in the valley, and they were very dry. He said to me, "Mortal, can*

these bones live?" I answered, "O Lord God, you know." Then he said to me, "Prophesy to these bones, and say to them: O dry bones, hear the word of the Lord. Thus says the Lord God to these bones: I will cause breath to enter you, and you shall live. I will lay sinews on you, and will cause flesh to come upon you, and cover you with skin, and put breath in you, and you shall live; and you shall know that I am the Lord."

— Ezekiel 37:1-6

I believe that on that day long ago, and in my many experiences, God spoke to me; he breathed new life into my bones. Just as God added tendons, flesh, and skin to transform the dead into the living, for me he provided a new spirit and a new way of seeing, following a powerful, painful experience that revealed my shallowness and misdirection. It was a difficult time for me, but because of it I learned much about God's plan and his love for me. Even Jesus was not spared the pain of this world. Yet, God loved him and was with him during his suffering.

Henry Drummond, a Scottish evangelist, spoke on the need for such difficult, yet transforming, experiences in life. "Do not isolate yourself. Be among people and among things, and among troubles, difficulties, and obstacles." Then, it is your choice as to how you will face your hardships. God will always love you, but he gives you the choice: Will you turn to him and accept his love and strength?

Thus, in looking back, there is no way I can regret that day. How can we regret the difficulties that shape our character or teach us? How can we deny God's loving and wise plan for us, even though that path may contain its share of obstacles? I am thankful for a plan that put me on a new and holy path, but when I speak of this new direction and a deepening of my mind and heart, what exactly do I mean? How does this apply to my role as a teacher?

In the years since, I have learned lessons and gathered and implemented ideas in my classroom; these I will share with you. However, this book first focuses on one primary epiphany. That is, my experience that day and all the many days following have taught me a supremely powerful lesson. In fact, it is the *ultimate lesson* for human beings that Paul wrote about in his letter to the Corinthians:

> *If I speak in the tongues of mortals and of angels, but do not have love, I am a noisy gong or a clanging cymbal.... Love never ends. But as for prophecies, they will come to an end; as for tongues, they will cease; as for knowledge, it will come to an end.... And now faith, hope, and love abide, these three; and the greatest of these is love.* — 1 Corinthians 13:1, 8, 13

It may seem absurdly simple, but of course, it is the elusive lesson the world needs most: "Love your neighbor as yourself."

Jesus, the ultimate teacher, modeled God's love. Jesus wasn't called to simply like or care for us. Incredibly, he was asked to sacrifice his life for us to prove the power of God's love for his people. Therefore, Jesus' sacrifice on the cross can be viewed as the ultimate lesson plan. His life and his death reveal the ultimate moral path: sacrifice that flows from a loving heart. He is our role model. He is the world's teacher. Now that we have been shown the way, how can we who are also teachers be content to strive for less than to love our students as Jesus loves us?

Therefore, in this book I will do two things. First, I will continue to present the argument as to why teachers must endeavor to love all of their students, why love should lie within each educator. I am quite sure I need to do this, as I believe I will encounter many readers who firmly believe that love does not need to be part of their lesson plans. They most likely think it is fine to plan and execute a semester's worth of material on their subjects without making conscious, active love the priority of their plans. Throughout the world, I'm sure millions of educated, skilled teachers are at this very moment planning for their next classes. They have wisely made a list of their objectives, attempting to comply with various mandates, including their own. Yet, when looking over the lists, how many of them have this as their very first objective: "Love my students as God loves me."

Shouldn't this goal be at the top of every list? And yet, as I said, I am sure that many educators have their reasons for not buying into such a belief. Maybe they will consider the words of Mahatma Gandhi, who said, "It is unwise to be too sure of one's own wisdom. It is healthy to be reminded that the strongest might weaken and the wisest might err." Hopefully, those who believe it is fine to teach and lead without love "might weaken" and be interested in developing a new view that places God's love first and then actively seeking ways in which they can *express* that love to students. This is something I have been working at for fifteen years — developing concrete ways to express love. I share my ideas in Section Two: "Twelve Love Lessons For Teachers."

I implore you: Be open to a new way of thinking, a new way of seeing your role as a teacher — God's way. Charles Dickens said, "A loving heart is the truest wisdom." Become wise and let new life be breathed into your dry bones. Help fulfill Ezekiel's vision: "They came to life and stood up on their feet — a vast army." Help create a more loving, miraculous world by letting your head and heart hear a new message, one of love and demonstration of that love for all God's people and for your students. Imagine a world in which all students are loved and learn in that loving environment. Wouldn't that be awesome? Think of all the lives that would be changed! The miracles unleashed! I hope I am not overreaching to imagine such a world. Just think of it! A world in which all students, all people, are instructed and treated with God's love. What would that world look like? It's an amazing thought!

Do you still think love is not necessary in the classroom? Then learn from Mother Teresa, someone infinitely wiser than I am. As a result of her worldly travels and countless interactions with God's people, she observed this simple yet world-changing truth: "There is more hunger for love and appreciation in this world than for bread." Today's students are hungry for love. We need to start feeding them. Yet, as always, you have a choice. What path will you travel at the fork in the road? The road well traveled by many but lacking in God's spirit and love? Or, will you venture down God's miraculous road that, to quote Robert Frost, too often in this world "want(s) wear"?

A New Road, A New Vision

One does not see anything until one sees its beauty.
— Oscar Wilde

As I began traveling down this new road, I became aware of various parallels. The consuming love I felt for my infant daughter is the same love God feels for me. He made me, and he loves me. God also loves my daughter with this same intensity. Thus, every child is his child, and every child is his special gift to humanity — his miracle. Remember Einstein's words? "There are only two ways to live your life. One is as though nothing is a miracle. The other is as though everything is a miracle."

My daughter was a miracle to me, as all children are to their parents. Often, the birth of a child encourages this new way of seeing: Every child is God's miracle, and therefore it is his or her birthright to be loved. When this realization began to wash over me, I started to look at everyone differently. Every human being, I now saw, is of the divine. Therefore, we are all related. The song "One" by the band, U2, powerfully declares this point. Look up the lyrics online. They are very powerful.

As the song points out, we are all "one blood." But recognizing that is not enough. Because of our shared humanity, you and I must do what we should. But what is that? What are you and I expected to do? Isn't it enough to be a good teacher? To be educated, motivated, and prepared? Remember when I asked you if it was over the top to imagine a world in which all students were taught with love? I said it was an amazing thought, one that is almost incomprehensible. Yet, to even inch toward that goal of world love, we must begin somewhere — ourselves — as Gandhi told us: "Be the change you want to see in the world."

Unfortunately, my experience as a teacher has shown me that many teachers either do not have a vision of themselves as instruments for creating a more loving world or are not revealing their love in the classroom as effectively as they might. Furthermore, some may wish to wield their influence in more life-changing ways but lack the tools to make their vision reality. There are those who have become cynical and unloving, and like Ezekiel are in need of a new spirit.

In my years of teaching, while I have encountered many fine teachers, I also have encountered several dry bones who do not see their students' beauty. One lady, a nice enough person to encounter at the copy machine or staff coffee pot, would often make derogatory comments about her students. One line stands out sharply. "Oh, they're a bunch of idiots," she exclaimed one morning. "They can't learn anything." I left the room shaking my head. Another teacher is rumored to scream at her college students. Also, in my earlier years of teaching at a high school, I would, from time to time, hear contemptuous comments in the staff lounge at lunchtime, derogatory words like, "Boy, that Carl is a real jerk. I don't know what's going to become of that kid."

When I hear such comments, I am reminded of Jesus addressing arrogance and judgment. When speaking to the smug members of a crowd, people who saw themselves as morally superior to the Samaritan adulterer, Jesus, in his well-known reply, admonished: "Let anyone among you who is without sin be the first to throw a stone at her" (John 8:7b). Of course, Jesus was the only one there who had the moral authority to throw a stone, as he was the only person there who was without sin. Did Jesus throw that stone? No. Jesus, through his words, revealed the face of God to us — one of forgiveness and compassion, not judgment and scorn.

Jesus also provoked those who viewed themselves as superior to their neighbors with, "Why do you see the speck in your neighbor's eye, but do not notice the log in your own eye?" (Matthew 7:3). When you begin to have a new view, one that holds that we are all brothers and sisters, how than can you not love your students? And how can you be transfixed on their shortcomings and look down on them, when you also are one of the beautiful miracles that God has created, a creation that is saved only by God's grace?

Unfortunately, for some, their arrogance becomes ideology, leading them to constantly view their students darkly, almost with a level of contempt. Too many teachers cling to negative views:

"Today's children don't care. Today's children are shallow and materialistic. Today's children are lazy." But is this true? Or do these views reflect back on the teacher, revealing a closed mind and a dark heart that has less to do with the reality of the students but much more with the teacher's unloving spirit? You might reply, "Well, thank goodness that is not me! I would never view my students that way." Maybe not. But be sure to look for the log in your own eye regularly. If we are going to remain capable of love, we need to shine light on our own unloving thoughts and behaviors that may surface from time to time. We also need to keep our ears and eyes open for God's truths.

In Matthew, Jesus attempted to teach a truth to the crowd, yet the people were stubborn. Jesus explained, "... seeing they do not perceive, and hearing they do not listen.... You will indeed listen, but never understand, and you will indeed look but never perceive. For this people's heart has grown dull" (Matthew 13:13b, 14b-15a). How many teachers have become calloused so that they cannot hear and learn a transforming message? I would tell them: Don't you realize that it is your privilege to even know your students? Don't take for granted your bounty. You've been given a great gift — the opportunity to touch someone's life and in turn be touched by all the gifts he or she has to offer. Do you recognize this? The Bible tells us, "For where your treasure is, there your heart will be also" (Matthew 6:21).

It is up to you to choose to travel a new road with a different vision. In other words, decide today that you and every one of your students is a miracle from God. Thus, treasure your students, see their beauty, and recognize them for the joyous gifts they are, honoring them by perceiving their talents and nurturing them to their individual miracles. Every student is gold! Our job is to polish.

Don't be stubborn and blind to the riches that are your students. It's funny, but when you become aware of a truth, you begin to see strands of it everywhere. Recently at church, our closing hymn, which I've sung many times, sparked my attention with its ending lines:

Here I am, Lord. Is it I, Lord?
I have heard you calling in the night.
I will go, Lord, if you lead me.
I will hold your people in my heart.[1]

Isn't time you truly held your students in your heart?

---

1. "Here I Am, Lord," words and music by Dan Schutte, 1981. Used by permission.

Love Isn't For Couch Potatoes: The Labor Of Love

Love does not dominate, it cultivates. — Goethe

Don't judge each day by the harvest you reap, but by the seeds you plant. — Robert Louis Stevenson

God has revealed in many ways his desire for us to love each other, to hold his people "in our hearts." With his help, we can learn to plant love in our classrooms and grow it day by day, spreading it far beyond our own walls. This is how we become the change we want to see in the world. Dr. James Dobson, leader of *Focus on Family*, spoke of the importance of loving students and laboring on love, which can cultivate great rewards.

> *I was only 25 at the time, and I* fell in love *with 250 science and math students. When I left to accept other responsibilities I fought back the tears.... We, as adults, must never forget the pain of trying to grow up and of the competitive world in which many adolescents live today. Taking a moment to listen, to care, and to direct such a youngster may be the greatest investment of a lifetime.*[1]

I appreciate Dobson's comments because I believe it is not enough to like students. Instead, we must endeavor to love all of our students. To simply have occasional warm feelings is to fall short of Christ's model. Yet, what exactly is love? We speak of it all the time, but do we really grasp what it is? If we don't, how can we consciously and effectively teach with love? One dictionary describes love in various ways. It is called a "strong affection for another rising out of kinship or personal ties." But I prefer one of its other definitions: "*unselfish* loyalty and *benevolent* concern for the good of another." This definition seems more apt. To be unselfish is to put another's success ahead of your own self-centeredness. Moreover, to have a benevolent concern for someone who is not your kin or personally known to you takes a love for humanity, a selfless tendency to advance the good of others because it is the highest moral path — God's desire.

Merriam-Webster's Dictionary also describes love as a verb. It describes the action of love as "to feel" or "cherish." It is the next definition that intrigues me: "*to like actively*." It does not say simply to like. It says to like *actively*. How is love achieved by liking actively?

The dictionary defines active as "moving, doing, or functioning" and "engaged in activity." This suggests that love requires action. Many books and articles on marriage also argue that love is not a noun but a verb. They argue that love takes work and commitment — doing. You actually have to get up off that couch and labor at love. Perhaps that is why I have trouble with the word "fall" in the phrase "fall in love." Falling suggests some sort of accident, like not planning to love but finding oneself swept up in an unexpected and irresistible sea of emotion. Of course, this happens. Teachers "fall in love" with that witty class clown or highly intelligent quiz-bowl kid. Maybe a particular student is similar to ourself, so we instinctively draw near. Doesn't everyone have his or her pet?

But what of the difficult students? The moody, the angry, or the low-achieving student? Will we "fall" in love with them? Probably not. Instead, we may find ourselves naturally disliking those students and distancing ourselves from them — those who need love the most! In sharing her own struggle, Saint Therese of Lisieux spoke on the need to constantly battle our negative impulses and instead consciously strive to *do* the loving work of Christ.

There is one sister in the community who has the knack of rubbing me the wrong way at every turn; her mannerisms, her ways of speaking, her character strike me as unlovable. But then she's a [sister]; God must love her dearly; so I am not going to let my natural dislike of her get the best of me. Thus, I remind myself that [Christian] love is not a matter of feelings; it means doing things. I have determined to treat this sister as if she is the person I love best in the world. Every time I meet her, I pray for her, and I offer [thanks] to God for her virtues and her efforts. I feel certain that Jesus would like me to do this.[2]

As Lisieux reveals, love should not be arbitrary or dependent upon personal feelings. Instead, love is "doing things" — a constant striving to love everyone. Lisieux used the word *determined*. Thus, instead of leaving love up to chemistry, admiration, mood, or chance, teachers should enter the classroom with the clear mindset that they will work hard and do what is necessary to love every single student by planting and allowing God's Holy Spirit and love to flow and grow in their classrooms.

---

1. James Dobson, *The Complete Marriage And Family Home Reference Guide* (Carol Stream, Illinois: Tyndale House, 2006).

2. Saint Therese of Lisieux, *Story of a Soul: The Autobiography of St. Therese of Lisieux*, 3rd edition (Washington DC: ICS Publications, 1996).

The Seed That "Never Faileth"

What is the kingdom of God like? And to what should I
compare it? It is like a mustard seed that someone took
and sowed in the garden; it grew and became a tree,
and the birds of the air made nests in its branches.
— Luke 13:18-19

Think back to the teacher who really seemed to love you. Can
you remember one? When I consider all of the many teachers who
taught me through elementary school, high school, college, and
graduate school, there are only three teachers who come strongly
to my mind as truly teaching me with love.

In the seventh grade, Mr. Miller, my science teacher, sent a
typed note home to my parents. I remember taking the official letter from the mailbox and slowly walking it into the house as I stared
at the envelope's return address: Lake Fenton Junior High.

Was I in trouble? Was I failing science?

I handed the letter to my mother. Suddenly, as she began reading Mr. Miller's words, a huge smile spread across her face. My
teacher had sent home a letter to sing my praises! It was full of
kindness and appreciation.

Incredibly, some thirty years later, I still have this letter. It had
a place of importance in my young life, and in 1977 I taped the
letter and envelope into a large yellow scrapbook among my blue
ribbons and cherished photographs. This is what Mr. Miller's letter said:

Dear Mr. and Mrs. Stevens,
I am Wendy's 7th grade Science teacher this year,
and I would like to let you know that thus far I have
certainly enjoyed having Wendy in class. All too often
the communications from school are of a negative na-
ture; however, when I have a student as friendly and
pleasant as Wendy, I like to let the parents know that I
appreciate it. Wendy always seems to be prepared for
class, and I am sure her grade will reflect this fact.

43

Thank you again for having a pleasant, well-mannered daughter.

Sincerely,
Joe Miller

Mr. Miller also sent copies of this letter to the principal and school counselor.

Who does this?

It is clear to me now that Mr. Miller was a teacher who taught with love. With love in his heart, he was able to not only see the unique miracles of me, but compelled to actively express them — a generous act. He did not have to do this. I'm sure as a teacher, track coach, father, and husband, Mr. Miller was a very busy man. Yet, on February 8, 1977, this busy teacher pulled up a chair, put a piece of paper in a typewriter, gathered up his loving thoughts about me, and composed and typed a heartfelt letter. This was before easy access to a computer, so he probably wrote a draft or two before he typed it. Mr. Miller even used whiteout correction fluid to fix a mistake so he would send home a perfect letter. Then, I imagine, Mr. Miller walked the letter to the school copy machine, where he made copies for the principal and school counselor. Finally, he folded the letter, placed it in an envelope, and gave it to the secretary to mail. Maybe he even mailed it himself.

And why? Nothing or no one required this of him. He wasn't receiving any pay or staff recognition. No one besides me, my family, and a few staff members ever knew he did it. What caused him to go beyond what was required, to make that effort and show me love that I still feel to this day?

As I said, that was some thirty years ago. Much of what he taught me about the solar system or photosynthesis, though clearly important, seems a bit fuzzy now. I can't exactly remember how a plant turns sunlight into food, or the precise order of the planets in our universe, yet the words I read that day and the love he showed me in class I can recall immediately. They touched me profoundly.

Clearly, love matters.

Clearly, love for students is of the utmost importance, as it has the power to transform lives forever.

The apostle Paul wrote that love "always perseveres." He revealed to us that all things pass away — prophecies, tongues, even knowledge — but "love never fails." Furthermore, Drummond, in his meditation, asked, "Can you tell me anything that is going to last?"

> *The wisdom of the ancients, where is it? It is wholly gone. You put yesterday's paper in the fire. Its knowledge has vanished away. You buy the old editions of the great encyclopedias for a few dollars. Their knowledge has vanished away.... At every workshop you will see, in the backyard, a heap of old iron, a few wheels, a few levers, a few cranks, broken and eaten with rust. Years ago that was the pride of the city. People flocked in from the country to see the great inventions; now they are superseded, their day is done. And all the boasted science and philosophy of this day will soon be old.[1]*

Yet, love will never be old, will never be superseded, will never be forgotten. Love, like a mighty stone cast upon a lake, makes a consequential splash whose powerful, spirited waves reverberate to every shore. Its power never ends. It is like the tiny mustard seed mentioned in the Bible, that once planted will continue to grow into a strong tree. John W. Schlatter, in *Chicken Soup for the Soul*, also wrote of the power of love, which he compares to a mighty building. "An architect knows if he builds with care, his structure may stand for centuries. A teacher knows that if he builds with love and truth, what he builds will last forever."

As I said, there are a few teachers I recall who stand out to me as teaching with love, as their treatment of me left a profound impression. A few years after the seventh grade, I was in another science class. That science teacher, a bespectacled Mr. Cupal, also showed me that classroom love is powerful and its impact endures.

One spring morning (it always seems to be spring — a time of rebirth?), Mr. Cupal called me to the front of his class; it was my senior year of high school. I had been in his freshman science course but done poorly due to too much talking and goofing off. Now, in my final semester, I was an A student. I slowly walked to the front

45

of the room, past glass beakers and microscopes, wondering why I was being singled out. As I quietly faced my curious classmates, I remember hearing the well-spoken Mr. Cupal say, "When I first had Wendy in class, she wasn't much of a student. She liked to talk all the time and flirt a lot. I have seen a new Wendy in my class this semester. She has shown what you can do if you put your mind to something. I must say that I am very proud of her." In addition to his words were the warmth of his smile and a kindness that radiated from him. It was a genuine love I had felt all semester long but was intensified in that moment as he shined his light on me.

To this day, I still vividly recall that moment and how proud I felt. I had never been recognized publicly before for academic achievement. I stood there full of pride and joy. I can still recall the feeling: It was like a new bright light was filling up all of me — love! Mr. Cupal, though he didn't have to, showed me love that day. He was kind, generous, unselfish, and sincere. He thought about me specifically and saw my efforts and need for validation. Thus, he made a conscious decision to lift me up, to do something benevolent.

That was a powerful, pivotal moment for me. Before that, I had often perceived myself as a class clown; I made people laugh to get attention, to fill my needs. I didn't see myself as academic or capable. Yet Mr. Cupal's words illuminated for me a new vision of myself. He planted a seed of hope and belief, and I began to see myself as someone with talent, with intelligence, perhaps even a college student. This was the miracle he helped create. Within days, I sought out the school counselor as I had begun considering going to college. I now have a master's degree. Mr. Cupal's actions that day made a profound mark. On that day, he went beyond what was required, and his mustard seed is still growing.

Besides Mr. Miller and Mr. Cupal, there are few teachers I recall as having that kind of effect on me. Of course, I encountered many fine teachers, educators who were bright, challenging, and skilled. Some were aloof; others more friendly. As we all know, education is a mixed bag. You experience many different teachers, each with his or her own beliefs, methods, and personality. Add the fact that college and graduate school can be a tough business, with top students competing for grades, attention, and approval. Often, in the large college classes that permeate most universities (and even the small), many teachers never even know their students' names, let alone love them or show that they love them.

Yet, in that often impersonal environment, I had one professor, Carrie Johnson, who taught at Michigan State University. Carrie was another teacher who, by her actions, seemed to truly love her students. When I or others would talk, she would look at us intently and listen closely. She was kind and patient. When I was finished speaking, she would offer praise and encouragement. I can picture her nodding her head thoughtfully, as if I had said something really worthy of her time and consideration. She also was generous. Of course, it didn't hurt that she brought bagels and cream cheese to every class! It showed she thought of our needs.

She also smiled and laughed a lot. She would even give a warm touch now and then, and often walk out of the class with me to continue talking about some comment I had made. Usually, she sat back and listened to us, posing thought-provoking questions and providing insightful comments every now and then. She trusted us to learn because it was clear she thought highly of us. She was courteous, too. In class or in her comments on our assignments, she was never mean, derogatory, or condescending.

She also saw the good in us, the miracles in us, and pointed them out, while showing us how we could improve even more. Now that so much time has passed, I sometimes have a difficult time precisely recalling her face. Yet, her demeanor is still so vivid in my mind and heart. She gave love to me, and her love inspired me to be my best. I went on to earn straight *A*s in graduate school. I know she played an enormous part. Carrie also had such a loving, generous spirit that she would invite all of us graduate students into her home for a party at the end of the school year. Who does that?

One May day, at the end of my studies at MSU, Carrie and I walked across the blooming campus and had lunch at a local gathering spot on Grand River. Her warm, smiling face was right at home among the blossoming tulips and daffodils that dotted campus. That afternoon Carrie talked to me like a friend, and I loved her for it. I will never forget the manner in which she validated me, making me feel worthy and special. Carrie made me feel loved, and she forever became one of my most cherished mentors.

Just recently, I read a *Reader's Digest* article about the Academy Award-winning actress Halle Berry. When Berry was a young girl, her mother decided to remove her from her urban school and place her in a suburban setting. In the piece, Berry reveals what a difficult time she had. She was one of a few people of color in her new school, and with this sudden change she experienced many negative feelings. She admits she began to go down the wrong path until she met a special teacher, a teacher who, Berry says, "loved" her. Not liked her, not cared for her, not taught her — Berry's own words were that this teacher *loved* her. That's a powerful claim. How many people can say they were loved by a teacher?

Looking back, Berry attributes much of her positive change at that time to this woman. As we all know, Berry went on to fulfill the awesome potential God provided her. Yet, is it reasonable to wonder what miracles would have remained dark if not for the love of that one teacher? How might Berry's life unfolded without that love?

When I think back to my early career in teaching, I ask, "Did I do that for my students, those students who wrote that nasty letter all those years ago? Did I make them feel that way? Was I patient, kind, and generous — loving?" In other words, did I plant love in that classroom, knowing that love "never faileth," and that my actions could have profound and far-reaching effects on my students' lives? Did I show my students that I loved them? Did I make them feel special, unique, meaningful, talented, or worthy? Did I honor Mr. Miller, Mr. Cupal, and Carrie Johnson by spreading the love they had shown me? Did I *do*? Or did I, confident in the supreme worth of my lesson plans, let my students sit there day after day, filled with their doubts and insecurities, their fears and past failings, their hunger not for bread but for validation and love, all the while waiting for me to lift them up while echoing God's words to Jesus: "You are my Son, whom I love; with you I am well pleased." Did I do this?

1. Henry Drummond, *The Greatest Thing in the World* (Uhrichsville, Ohio: Barbour and Company, Inc., 1994).

Hungry Hearts

"I love you. I am pleased with you." Do we ever stop hungering for this message in our own lives? No! We all crave love and acceptance. How many times have we sung along, with heads nodding, to Bruce Springsteen's song lyrics, "Everybody's got a hungry heart"? Many people argue that this need for love is life's primary focus. Albert Einstein observed, "Hunger, love, pain, fear are some of those inner forces which rule the individual's instinct for self-preservation."

Our students, like everyone, have hungry hearts needing love. Often we teachers are too blinded, indifferent, competitive, self-protective, overworked, or unbelieving to notice or care. Our own needs and beliefs cloud our ability to envision a new perspective and path.

When I became a college English instructor, I had a decidedly different view than when I began as a high school teacher. As described earlier, when I was a beginning teacher I was mostly concerned with me — my syllabus, my lesson plans. Of course, I cared that my students learned. Like most teachers, I worked hard at becoming an effective instructor. I applied the various theories on which I had been schooled. Yet something was missing, something no one talks about. However, with time, experience, and Christ's Spirit in me, I realized I wasn't truly trying to emulate Christ's example; therefore, I didn't have intimacy with my students. Without love, I didn't have a real connection.

Looking back, I'm reminded of the television show, *ER*. In that television drama, people are constantly wheeled through the hospital doors with the most grotesque and painful conditions — gunshot wounds, infections, diseases — you name it. But oftentimes, while they are treating these suffering patients, the doctors laugh amongst themselves. They flirt with the new interns and bicker over bad relationships, all while the hurting patient is only inches away, anguishing.

Actually, the patients are often not the focal point of the story at all. Instead, these television doctors' lives are portrayed as far more interesting. From watching the show, you get the idea that these health professionals don't need to be close to their patients to do a good job. In some ways, it's an assembly line of human suffering. Anonymous people are wheeled in, tended to, and discharged, all without a human connection forged between the caregiver and the sufferer. Of course, you might argue, this is just a television show. This is not real life. This is just an exaggeration.

However, watching this show has sparked a few thoughts about real life. The first is that people might become indifferent to those they serve because the work becomes tedious and monotonous. Over time, people might become somewhat like products on an assembly line. Thus, it becomes easy to tune out, or just to go through the motions. The second thought is that becoming intimate with people calls for risk. When you begin to care, your empathy opens you up to many feelings, some of which are painful, and responsibilities, most of which are hard. Maybe it's easier just to stay emotionally isolated. When you don't care too much, not much is expected of you, right? The third thought is that some people might believe that intimacy is not required in order to do a good job. The doctor might argue that he needs no level of closeness with his patient in order to heal him. If he can tend to the patient's wound, isn't that enough?

Similar to those lines of thinking, I believe I too kept my distance from my students when I first began teaching. Oh, I was friendly enough. I participated in all the events designed to persuade students I was one of the friendly faculty. As a high school teacher, I even kissed a baby pig on the gym floor in front of the entire student body! Didn't that count for something? After school, I helped with homecoming and snowcoming activities that involved shaving cream and pies in the face. Here and there I might have helped a particularly needy student. But overall, my game plan was to devise a solid syllabus and execute it well, day to day, week to week. That's why I was hired — so I thought. Emulating Christ in order to forge close, loving relationships with my students was not on my master plan. Yes, in class I was friendly, funny, and enthusiastic. And I taught well. That seemed enough.

However, as my awareness of Christ and my love for Christ deepened, I began to discover a new awareness about my teaching and my students. I also began to feel a profound and expanded love for people around me. As I explained earlier, my view of humanity shifted. My pupils were no longer simply learners of a particular subject; instead they were my sisters and brothers — God's miracles in his kingdom.

This view is markedly different. The love and care I would bestow upon my own brother and God's child is far greater than the affection I once held for my students. I would argue that this greater affection is crucial if a teacher is going to truly touch people's lives in a long-lasting, meaningful way, one that empowers them, lifts them up, and helps fill them with confidence and love for life's journey — miraculous transformations. Of course, teachers can strive for much less and often do. But is that what God wants from us? To do less with his gifts? Is this the model Christ gave us?

Once this shift began taking place in me, this transformation of my worldview, I began to desire a deeper, more meaningful relationship with my students. I believed that my teaching could become more powerful and more profound if I taught lovingly to individuals.

But what were their needs? I knew they were all sitting before me to learn the fundamentals deemed necessary to pass my English course. We would focus on paragraphs, essays, and research papers. But should I only focus on what is deemed language arts? What about focusing on students? Where should the emphasis be placed in the classroom — on the subject matter or the person? This is something you need to think about. For some teachers, the subject is God.

What or whom do you serve? Christ washed the feet of his disciples. It was clear he served humankind. How then can I do less? How can I as a teacher ignore the needs and hungers of my students? Am I not there to serve them? How can their miracles be planted and grown when they are hungry for nurturing?

I liken it to this. You're sitting in a room. You haven't eaten in a long time. All you can think about is food — the smell of it, the taste of it. Your mouth salivates at the thought of your last meal.

53

Not only does your stomach ache for sustenance, but your entire body feels weak. You're apathetic, irritable, haggard, and listless. You begin to withdraw; your growth becomes stunted. Clearly, you are not taking in enough nutrients for the maintenance of life. How many of our students sit before us hungry, even *starving*? How many of them are craving understanding, acceptance, advice, confidence, validation, peace, or even love?

While you sit there in that room, malnourished and ravenous for all that eludes you, all that you need to thrive, your teacher, this wise, educated academic, begins to instruct you on the importance of the possessive apostrophe. Of course apostrophes are important. They let us know we are God's people. Yet, at that moment, it's all you can do to keep your head up.

Do I exaggerate? Perhaps. I do, however, have proof of the needs before us — my students' letters. When I experienced this change in my thinking and my growing love for my students, I began asking them for letters. To me, letters are personal. They say to people, "I care enough to read your personal thoughts and help you." Also, perhaps I wanted to replace that nasty letter from years ago with some new letters, words of hope and kindness. At the beginning of each semester and at the end of each fifteen-week semester, I ask my students for letters.

In the first-day-of-class letters, students write about their home lives, friends, jobs, and pets. But, astonishing to me at first, they also write candidly about their fears and hurts. They often tell me about the obstacles in their lives, their past failures, and the problems at home. It seems clear to me that they want someone to know that they are hungering inside, and in some cases, starving. Perhaps, just perhaps, I might be a person willing to help them, even love them.

Later, at the end of the class, the students mostly write about the ways in which I did indeed love them and nurture them. I know from their comments that love is more important to students than anything else the teacher has to offer. In the Appendix of this book, I include excerpts from many student letters that confirm this belief: We first hunger for love. The American food writer, M. F. K.

Fisher, who recognized that the human hunger for love, food, and security is completely intertwined, wrote: "When I write of hunger, I am really writing about love and the hunger for it, and the warmth and the love of it. And then the warmth and richness and fine reality of hunger satisfied ... and it is all one."[1]

So what do students hunger for? The comments that follow were extracted from first-day letters from just two classes, some 58 or less students. From the many semesters I have taught college English, I have read hundreds of these letters, so these are just a portion. Also, as I said, these letters reveal only comments made at the beginning of the course. Thus, they only skim the surface of what students will reveal to me as the semester unfolds. Keep in mind that they didn't even know me; it was the first day of class! Yet, I believe they quickly felt comfortable expressing themselves honestly to me; they could sense the Holy Spirit in the room, which filled it with love. Of course, many of my students are not suffering. Yet, they still hunger for love and validation. Many others, however, reveal by their letters just how they long for kindness, sincerity, and generosity — some of the ingredients of love.

As the course progresses, I continue to work at creating a trusting, loving environment, so naturally my students reveal more and more to me. Before I share these anonymous excerpts with you, I'll provide you with some of my students' salutations that began letters that were sometimes cheery, sometimes anxious — such a mixed bag! Regardless of the tone, all of them touched me. As you look them over and perceive their humor and sweetness, you'll perhaps begin to see the miracles I see. And you may be encouraged to ask the question I asked myself: "How could I not love them?"

> *Dear Windy ... My Dear Wendy ... Dear Mrs. Wendy Byard ... hello Wendy (with a smiley face) ... What Up Wendy ... hey Wendy ... Dearest Wendy ... Hiya Wendy ... Good Morning Wendy ... My Dearest Wendy*

Even something as seemingly transparent as the beginning of a letter can reveal the personalities and emotions of human beings.

Immediately, I was touched by the special qualities, the miraculous nature of each student. Then I read the remainder of their letters and found them to be even more touching and often so candid. In the next chapter are some anonymous excerpts I have saved over the past years. Please read them all even though they repeat certain feelings and themes. I think it's important to realize how universal certain needs are. As I read them again, I wonder: How can teachers turn a blind eye to their students' need for love?

1. M. F. K. Fisher, *Stay Me, O Comfort Me: Journals and Stories, 1933-1941* (New York: Knopf Publishing Group, 1995).

What My Students' Letters Reveal

Although this list of student comments may seem long, I would like you to read and think deeply about them. What do they make you think and feel? If these were your students, how would you respond? *Should* you respond?

- I'm really rusty ... writing is not my strong point. As one of my teachers put it, "You're the queen of bullshit."
- I'm not the smartest person in the world.
- I don't think I'm very funny.
- I'm a very boring person.
- I'm not the best reader, writer, and speller.
- I fear like in high school I won't do good. I probably won't fail, but I will struggle.
- I am not very good at English.
- I did not do very good in high school.
- I am nervous about this class.
- I absolutely do not like speaking in front of people.
- I am a slow reader.
- First of all, I am not good at English. I've always struggled.
- I'll be honest, I hated English.
- English is my worst subject ... I have never liked English.
- I have never liked English. School has not been one of my strong points. I didn't really like it, so I didn't really apply myself.
- Unfortunately, my best is not always enuff. I am dyslexic and have strugeled with school my hole life. As I am shure you can tell my speling and writing is not the best.
- I went to six or seven different schools my whole life, and it was tough for me ... It is basically a boring life so far.
- Well to be honest with you, English was always my worst subject. I've always struggled to make the grade.
- It has been a very long time since I have been in school, so I am not sure what to expect.

57

- I have never been a big fan of English.
- I really don't think I am a good writer.
- I don't really enjoy English classes too much.
- I have heard the line, "You have no English talent" before ... In high school I wasn't the best English student.
- I can't spell for bears.
- I don't do that well when it comes to writing and reading.
- Arriving on campus that first day I was terrified, wondering if I was capable of achieving my educational objective.
- I've always had trouble with English ... I don't like to read books.
- [My brother] died in 1991 at age fourteen from a brain tumor.
- I'm not the best English student.
- English class has not always been my strong point.
- I know I will be overwhelmed once we get into the work.
- I am also very hyper most of the time and hate sitting still, so I might get antsy.
- I am having a hard time getting motivated.
- ... I played baseball and football, too. English on the other hand was not as well enjoyed. But I survived four years of it.
- I am an average English student. I have some problems with it ... I'm not much of a reader but that is probably because of my lack of interest in what I had to read ... I have a hard time with ideas.
- ... I'm not the best at writing papers and understanding literature. I have a hard time coming up with ideas to write about ... English is usually the hardest class for me. It's kinda difficult and I don't really enjoy it.
- This is a very scary road for me. I am afraid of failing at this.
- I can't stand presentations because I'm not really a people person.

- My main concern about starting college is having time to do my homework and work at the same time. In high school I did okay in English, but it definitely wasn't my favorite subject.
- I was not such a good student in high school.
- English was one of my worst subjects. I have always just been able to sweat by. My biggest area that I have problems with is writing, anything where I have to make my own, I just can't get rolling.

Unfortunately, these comments just skim the surface. As the class progresses and many essays are written and collected, so many more of their needs surface. Sometimes I can't believe what issues and needs gnaw at students. As I develop loving and deepening relationships with my students, they feel more trusting and begin revealing to me, in a variety of ways, the needs in their lives.

So, what needs and issues afflict some students so that they come to class with longings or heavy hearts? I think it's important to understand and acknowledge the unseen forces in students' lives that prevent them from learning fully the subject matter at hand and also keep them from reaching their full miraculous potentials in this world. Some needs are as simple as kindness and individual attention. However, in the years that I have been teaching I have found that many students have more pressing needs.

Here are some of the issues that my students have shared with me, issues that lead them to hunger for concern, confidence, information, advice, validation, healing, peace, and ultimately and most importantly, love.

- divorced parents
- abandonment by the father or mother or both
- never knew their mother or father
- sexual abuse by the father
- alcoholic parents
- addicted or past addiction to drugs
- girlfriend addicted to heroin and in rehab
- date rape in high school

- single parent
- brother-in-law shot dead over a gambling dispute
- older student returning to school
- forced abortion
- depression
- attempted suicide
- bipolar illness
- racial discrimination
- moving from town to town and school to school
- father fell asleep at the wheel, crashed, and died
- teen parent
- involved in car accident in which a relative died
- moved from the city to the country
- dyslexia
- autism
- sexual orientation discrimination and issues
- eating disorders
- sexual abuse by a relative
- bullied/attacked in high school
- pregnancy in high school
- marriage in high school
- divorce
- house foreclosed on
- lost a job
- uncaring parenting
- home destroyed by fire
- brother died of brain tumor
- fighting for child custody
- car accident
- facial disfigurement due to accident
- star athlete now relegated to *just another student*
- death of a baby
- violence at home

Whew. It's overwhelming, isn't it? The suffering of mankind? Yet, Socrates wisely perceived, "One word frees us of all the weight and pain in life. That word is love." He, of course, is not the first to teach us this truth. However, if you are still not convinced that love is the key to life and the most necessary ingredient to teaching, then consider the following chapter, which conveys the words of the ultimate teacher — Christ himself.

Christ Was Clear

I have attempted to present various arguments as to why teachers, various leaders, and *you* should love your students and actively endeavor to express that love in ways that help unleash the miracles in people's lives. The most powerful argument for love in the classroom is found in the examples and words of Christ, revealed to us by his life on Earth. For example, in a conversation with Simon Peter, Christ engaged in a series of questions and commands to teach Simon Peter what he wanted from him. Through careful analysis of the passage's nuances, many lessons can be learned. However, one lesson seems clear: Jesus wanted Simon Peter to go beyond fondness, beyond simple affection, beyond brotherly feelings. Instead, he wanted Simon Peter to know, feel, and spread a more powerful love to Christ's "lambs." Read the dialogue carefully.

> *When they had finished breakfast, Jesus said to Simon Peter, "Simon son of John, do you love me more than these?" He said to him, "Yes, Lord; you know that I love you." Jesus said to him, "Feed my lambs." A second time he said to him, "Simon son of John, do you love me?" He said to him, "Yes, Lord; you know that I love you." Jesus said to him, "Tend my sheep." He said to him the third time, "Simon son of John, do you love me?" Peter felt hurt because he said to him the third time, "Do you love me?" And he said to him, "Lord, you know everything; you know that I love you." Jesus said to him, "Feed my sheep."* — John 21:15-17

In Greek, different words exist for love: *agape* and *philio*. Notice they are both verbs. The definition of *agape* is to "love something dearly." However, the definition of the other word, *philio*, is "to like or be fond of something." Thus, Jesus is attempting to ascertain what type of love Simon has for Jesus — fondness or dear love. Is it enough that Simon is merely fond of Jesus; that he has simple "affection" for the Son of God? If so, what will that accomplish? How will simple affection allow Simon to do God's work and carry him through the tough days ahead, which ultimately includes the sacrifice of his own life?

Christ is attempting to determine if Simon Peter truly loves him and is thus up to the challenging task of being his disciple. Does Simon love Christ genuinely, with all his heart? If he does not, how can he possibly be full of love for those he is expected to shepherd? Is it enough for Simon to simply be fond of God's people? Again, no. If Simon's heart is shallow, he will not be able to tend and feed Christ's people as Christ desires.

Christ's own example is one of extreme sacrifice. He also asked for *agape* love and sacrifice from his followers. Once again, I argue that it is not enough to simply be fond of our students. Christ did not tell us to love people in the manner we wish to be loved. He did not tell us to love people in the manner we feel like loving them. No, Christ, who died for us, was quite clear as to the type of love he expects: "My command is this: Love as I have loved you." *Agape* love. To love *dearly*.

Are you finally convinced? Or are you at least toying with the idea that God wants you to love your students? Are you convinced that through his Holy Spirit, God will create classroom miracles in your students' lives? If so, great! Then the big question becomes: "What now?"

Section Two:

Twelve Love Lessons
For Teachers

Be Like Bo

I sat down for lunch one chilly November Friday when the phone rang. It was my husband, and his voice was tense.

"Have you been watching the news? They just announced that Bo Schembechler died."

His words shocked me. Bo Schembechler dead? The tough but beloved football coach of the University of Michigan Wolverines? Bo seemed too strong to die, too fiery, and too intense. Yes, he was 77, but he still represented grit and tenacity to thousands of his fans and players. In fact, just the day before his death, the ailing Schembechler addressed his much-loved Wolverines on the eve of their Michigan-Ohio State rivalry, telling the players once again to focus on "the team, the team, the team!"

I turned on the television, and every news report focused on this man, this great coach who, over 21 seasons, won thirteen Big Ten titles, never had a losing season, was the Big Ten Coach of the Year seven times, and led his team to seventeen bowl games, including ten Rose Bowls. It was only fitting that this football icon receive so much media coverage. In the days to come, Michigan media was saturated with highlights about Bo.

As I absorbed all these many glowing accounts, something began to surprise me — something I hadn't known or even expected. People loved Bo Schembechler. I knew people admired and appreciated him for his football prowess and success, but *loved* him? This demanding, no-excuses football coach given to sideline outbursts? In my mind's eye I could still recall the many Saturdays spent watching Bo pace the UM sidelines, face tight in a grimace, hands thrust deep in pockets. *Love* Bo? Yet, consider this event described by *The Grand Rapids Press* following Bo's death.

*During a Friday rally put on by **The Huge Show** on WBBL-AM (1340), fans of Michigan and Ohio State gave Bo Schembechler a one-minute standing ovation* *instead of a traditional moment of silence. Michigan fans repeatedly chanted "We love Bo."*[1]

On November 21, 2006, some 20,000 people attended a memorial for Bo at Michigan Stadium — 20,000 fans! Among them were the former coaches and the current coach, along with the entire staff of Ohio State University — Bo's biggest rival!

Over and over, I encountered such amazing sentiments and displays of respect and love.

Former Michigan State football coach, George Perles, said, "I am certainly going to miss him, I loved him." Perles also described a time when Bo signed autographs and took photos with mostly Michigan State Spartan fans, his other great rival. Perles said, "He got a standing ovation from all the Spartan fans. They loved him." Another news account described the feelings of a 1978 UM graduate: "I loved Bo. He was the reason I came here." Perhaps the following words best reveal the deep feeling so many had for Bo. They were spoken by Dan Horning, who served the coach as a student manager and went on to serve on the UM Board of Regents. "I'm stunned and very, very saddened over Bo's passing," Horning said. "My heart aches."

As I read these touching words about the deep feelings so many people had for Bo Schembechler, I wondered why. How was it that this seemingly tough, exacting football coach inspired such love and devotion in others? I could recall only a few similar public outpourings of feeling but none for such a hard-nosed football man. I began my research. I began poring over the media accounts, examining the various stories told by Bo's friends and players. What I found seems so simple, yet so seemingly rare in this world, whether it takes place on the football field or in a college classroom, something that God so wants for us. The reason that Bo Schembechler was so deeply loved was because he truly loved others. He followed Christ's commandment: "Love as I have loved you."

Schembechler, who attended St. Andrews Episcopal Church in Ann Arbor, practiced *agape* love. Again and again, Schembechler put others first: his *team*. The evidence shows that Schembechler, in addition to being a successful coach, was much, much more: a mentor and friend to many, loving people and connecting with people in a variety of ways, often deeply, to help empower and transform them, encouraging them to be their best. Consider the following examples taken from various news outlets:

> *Tom Slade, a 1971 UM quarterback, died from cancer shortly before Bo's death. Just before Slade died, Bo made time to be with him at his side.*[2]

> *Craig Mutch, a former UM linebacker, said, "I feel like I lost a dad, because Bo was like a second father to me. He taught all his players, and anyone who was around him, so much. He taught you how to be a man, to be on time, to do things the right way, that you were only as good as your word, how to be responsible, that you got exactly what you put into things ... he was a hell of a man."*[3]

> *Julia Moore, a 1991 Michigan graduate who was employed by the football recruiting office, said that Schembechler was like a father to her, wanting the best for her. Yes, he instructed her, but with love and from the heart.*[4]

> *James Humphries, a former football player, said that Bo was always kind and encouraging. He also was a man who stuck by his word.*[5]

> *Bo tried to help former player Michael Guy Smith, who was imprisoned for life under new life-without-parole legislation. In 1998, Bo asked the state parole board to free Smith.*[6]

> *Dan Horning, the student manager, said, "I learned more from him about life than any university professor."*[7]

> *Reporter Angelique S. Chengelis recalled that for one interview Bo bought scones for the two of them to share.*

It was a "simple gesture but one that meant a great deal."[8]

Mike Lantry, a former UM kicker, said, "He had a way to push you hard and to make you want to play as hard as you could possibly be pushed. Then, just after you had gone through the meat grinder of that day's practice, you'd walk out of the locker room together and he'd call you by your first name and want to know how your studies were going."[9]

James P. Hackett, a former player, remembered Bo, right before his death, as being more concerned about another past player who had cancer than his own health issues. "Bo was confirming with me how frustrated he was that we couldn't have found a match for him for a bone marrow transplant. It was just so perfect, as the week played out, that this was what was on his mind, taking care of somebody else. He was a true hero."[10]

"On the morning of my surgery, [Bo] called and when I woke up from surgery there was a big flower arrangement there from him," said Debbie Williams-Hoak, a UM track and field star. "I could go see him anytime and that made this female athlete feel real special ... When I think of all the wonderful things that have happened to me since I made that decision to come to Ann Arbor and the university, I will be forever grateful to Bo."[11]

In addition to all of Bo's many duties, he also devoted much of his time helping others by attending to the charity named after his wife Millie, who succumbed to cancer.[12]

The kind words and stories go on and on.

These many words and accounts paint a picture of a person who through word and deed, gestures small and sometimes great, touched the lives of countless people, creating miracles that will never be fully accounted for. And so often present in these people's remembrances of Bo is the word love. Bo loved his players, and they loved him. Bo made the choice and the effort, emotion becoming motion, to care deeply and actively about the people who crossed his path. As a result, it seems so many people went on to lead truly better lives — the miracles sparked by the love of one man.

As teachers, we should strive to be like Bo. I know, that's a tall order. But with our own lives and our own talents we should endeavor to love our students and then, through our words and deeds, make that love real to them, so that they, too, can experience miraculous changes in their lives. You don't have to be a Big Ten football coach to make a difference. You just have to care more than is required — then show it.

----

1. *The Grand Rapids Press*, "Seen and heards. Reactions to Bo's death," November 18, 2006.

2. *The Detroit News*, Phil Callihan, "A coach unlike any other — Bo's greatest gift was as a teacher and his way of reaching people," November 18, 2006.

3. *The Grand Rapids Press*, Howie Beardsley, "Coach is mourned by the many he mentored. He was seen as a father to the close family of UM football players, supporters," November 18, 2006.

4. *The Associated Press*, David Eggert, "Michigan Faithful Pay Respects to Schembechler," November 20, 2006.

5. *Ibid.*

6. *The Michigan Daily*, "Schembechler defends former player," October 16, 1998.

7. *Op cit, The Grand Rapids Press.*

8. *The Detroit News*, Angelique S. Chengelis, "Bo always mattered, wherever he was," November 12, 2007. Reprinted with permission from *The Detroit News*. Approved by Jon Wolman, Editor and Publisher.

9. *The Detroit News*, Fred Girard, "UM loses a legend — Intensity and integrity defined Wolverines great Schembechler, November 18, 2006. Reprinted with permission from *The Detroit News*. Approved by Jon Wolman, Editor and Publisher.

10. *Ibid*.

11. *The Ann Arbor News*, Geoff Larcom, "Behind scenes, Bo touched so many lives," November 20, 2006.

12. *Op cit, The Detroit News*.

Love Lesson #2

You Can't Show (Or Sow)
What You Don't Know

Sometimes, loving words and actions come naturally to people. But, as with anything important and worthwhile, we should pay close attention to and study that which matters. If we have made the decision to dedicating ourselves to loving our students, just what are we supposed to do? Bo Schembechler had many games, seasons, and years to show his players that he loved them. What can we teachers and mentors do in the time and settings available to us?

When I look back over my students' letters and essays and think about their human longings and issues, I know they cry out for a teacher to respond lovingly. The apostle Paul, in a letter to the Corinthians, spoke of the need of reflecting the living spirit of Christ in our lives:

> *You show that you are a letter of Christ, prepared by us, written not with ink but with the Spirit of the living God, not on tablets of stone but on tablets of human hearts.* — 2 Corinthians 3:3

So, once again, how do we follow Christ's loving example in the classroom and avoid being simply a "resounding gong or a clanging symbol"? First, I think it's extremely important to take a close look at what love is. I've argued that love takes work, that it is active and requires *doing*. But I think it may be worthwhile to have a more precise view as to what comprises love in order to more fully practice it. Once again, Drummond, in his meditation, provides excellent food for thought with this analogy on love.

> *As you have seen a scientist take a beam of light and pass it through a crystal prism, as you have seen it come out on the other side of the prism broken up into its*

73

*component colors — red, blue, yellow, violet, orange,
and all the colors of the rainbow — so Paul passes this
thing, love, through the magnificent prism of his own
intellect, and it comes out on the other side broken up
into its elements ... the spectrum of love.*[1]

According to Drummond's analysis of Paul's teachings, these are the *nine elements of love*:

Patience: "Love suffereth long."
Kindness: "And is kind."
Generosity: "Love envieth not."
Humility: "Love vaunted not itself."
Courtesy: "Doth not behave unseemly."
Unselfishness: "Seeketh not her own."
Good Temper: "Is not easily provoked."
Guilelessness: "Thinketh no evil."
*Sincerity: "Rejoiceth not in iniquity, but rejoiceth in
    the truth."*[2]

I believe that what I have been thinking, doing, and saying in my college classroom — my lesson plans for love — tries to reflect these loving ingredients. First, let me assure you that I am far from perfect. Like everyone, I have had days where I have been sick, tired, and uninspired. Yet, when in the classroom, I do try to put aside my own issues and concentrate on loving my students, as imperfect as I am. Paul, in his letter to the Corinthians, does not tell us to be perfect. Only God is perfect. Instead, he tells us to aim for perfection. Every day, in all we do, we should strive to model Jesus Christ's loving example.

Thus, in the classroom, we must keep these qualities of love before us, guiding us. We have a choice to make: How will we use our authority? To love and serve others? Or ourselves? An anonymous quote I read recently put it this way: "There are two ways of exerting one's strength: one is pushing down, the other is pulling up." The classroom is a place of service. It is not a place for me to exert my strength by pushing down. Instead, the teacher's strength should be used to pull others up. Booker T. Washington said, "If you want to lift yourself up, lift up someone else."

As I explained earlier, I have my students write letters to me at the close of the fifteen-week course. They are pretty darn honest about what they like and why. You might be thinking, "Of course they are going to tell you what you want to hear. Who's going to jeopardize his grade by being negative? Can you really trust what they have to say?" Well, all I can tell you is that I do trust what they say. I have gotten to know my students quite well over that time period, perhaps better than I know a lot of people. In our conversations and through their essays, we have forged brief but intense relationships. Perhaps I provide a safe, respectful, and loving place for them. I believe they know I love them, from all that I say and do, and because of that loving environment, many feel confident to express themselves freely and honestly.

What I have chosen to share in the following chapters and in the Appendix are the positive comments. They overwhelmingly outnumber the negative, which focus more on issues like "less work please" or "you need to number your course pack!" The positive comments reveal what my students appreciate about the loving environment I create for them. Some of the comments praise me. I do not share these to flatter myself, as I don't see their comments as being truly about me. When they are praising me, they are actually telling me what they liked about my attitude, beliefs, and behavior, all of which are my attempts to follow in Christ's footsteps, as flawed as I am.

In the upcoming chapters I will share with you excerpts from some letters my students wrote to me, and there are many. However, I believe their comments shine an extraordinary amount of light on what students need to feel loved so that their learning is elevated, their spirits are lifted, and their miracles unleashed. Thomas Wolfe, in *Look Homeward Angel*, wrote, "I am a part of all that I have touched and that has touched me." My students' comments show that they have indeed been touched, just as I have been touched by the blessing of knowing them. Through these people, these miracles, I believe I have come in contact with God.

I hope you find their words and my comments and ideas useful, whether you are a teacher or in some other leadership position. While we all fulfill different roles and are uniquely gifted, I believe we are all similarly called to one mission clearly articulated by Christ: "Love one another as I have loved you" (John 15:12).

---

1. Henry Drummond, *The Greatest Thing in the World* (Uhrichsville, Ohio: Barbour and Company, Inc., 1994).

2. *Ibid.*

Get Your Head On Straight

Are not two sparrows sold for a penny? Yet not one of them will fall to the ground apart from your Father. And even the hairs of your head are all counted. So do not be afraid; you are of more value than many sparrows.
— Matthew 10:29-31

Before you can begin meaningfully expressing love to students, you need to get your head on straight. What do you believe? Where are you coming from? What is your philosophy regarding why you are a teacher and to what ends? If you don't see your students as beautiful gifts from God, miracles from the almighty, then maybe it's time for a new view. But first, consider this. The Bible makes clear that God knows us so intimately that even the hairs on our head are numbered. It also makes clear, over and over, that God loves and values us.

Thus, as teachers, we should believe God loves and holds in great importance every one of our students. Further, if God places such importance on each individual human being, then it only follows he wants us to as well. Understanding this, I believe that it is my duty as God's servant to treat students as God would have them treated: by acknowledging and treating them as valuable and unique beings. To this end, I strive to create an environment in which students are singularly known and cared for — not as a class of students, not as people I'll get to know eventually, not as distant learning receptacles, but as divinity — godly creations who deserve individual love and service. Read below the comments of some of my students and perceive the joy they felt at being known and loved in my class.

- I was afraid that I would be known only as a number, but in your class I was on a first-name basis ... walking in to see your friendly face, a warm smile, and a handshake.

Out of all my college professors you are the most kind, friendly, and caring.

- In the beginning of the semester I could tell that as soon as I had walked in the door that it was going to be a very laid-back and caring class ... I have never had a teacher come up and properly introduce themselves to me. As soon as that happened I could tell that you were a very one-on-one teacher and that you cared about your students.

- It also makes a huge difference that you actually take the time to learn everyone's names rather than each of us just being thirty more students to you.

- The second I had stepped foot in your class I knew there was something special in the room. The way you lightened the class made us all feel so comfortable and worthwhile. You gave us individual attention, which one needs in order to feel a part of the class.

- I feel like you really care about your students. Most teachers never sit down and have a one-on-one conversation with their students. There were many times in the past semester that you sat down with each of us to make sure that we were on the right track.

- This was my first semester of college, and you made it an easy transformation for me. I can't thank you enough. As a student one of the things I will remember about your class is the one-on-one relationship you had with us.

- Anyway, now it is the end of the class. I feel as if we just got to know each other and already we must say good-bye.

- Another thing I like about you is you try and get to know all your students. I think that it is good to know your students. Then they might come and talk to you if they have a problem.

- Thanks for being a down-to-earth teacher and also a friend. You made it very comfortable for us to talk to you ... I like how you tried to get involved in our lives and really were interested in us. Thank you so much!

- You always tried to reach each student individually. This quality will always be with me because you took the time to listen and help us, even when you didn't have to. One thing that will always stick out in my mind are the many times that you would stay after class and help Alison and I with whatever we needed. Even after everyone else left, you stayed and explained things we didn't understand, or helped us to write better papers, and you never rushed us to get things done. Even if we wanted to stay an hour after class, you would have stayed that extra hour and made sure that we as students got the full benefit of your teaching. You even came to class and listened to us present even though there were only five of us there ... The fact that I can talk to you and you don't make me feel inferior to you is, in my opinion, what makes you an excellent teacher.

- I always felt I could talk to you if I ever needed to. It is nice to have teachers that care.

- You have a connection with the young students (which is almost everyone in the class!). When people connect like that I think it helps them want to do better.

- You helped me a lot with everything that is going on with me. I probably got more out of talking to you than just about anybody else.

- I am a fifty-year-old woman; I started in college ... after thirty years in a factory ... Arriving on campus the first day I was terrified, wondering if I was capable of achieving my educational objective. Sitting in the front row, I was greeted with a bright smile from Wendy Byard. Her friendly, caring, light-hearted teaching style soon had me calm and ready to learn. Wendy's attitude and willingness to help inspired me to overcome my reservations and excel in her class. I am very grateful that she was my first college instructor. She gave me confidence to continue on with my college education.

- I truly felt that you cared more than you were required to ... I believe characteristics like that is what makes good instructors great.

When the semester ends and I sit down to read these comments, I hope it doesn't make me seem overly emotional to reveal that when reading their words I sometimes cry. The joy they feel at being known and loved is so evident, and it deeply touches me. As a teacher, I have been entrusted with the power to create joy, trust, confidence, validation, and love. Morrie Schwartz, the teacher who suffered from ALS and became famous as the subject of *Tuesdays With Morrie*, said, "The culture we have does not make people feel good about themselves. And you have to be strong enough to say if the culture doesn't work, don't buy it."

I agree. Throughout my lifetime, I have found myself in various situations and environments that did not seem to operate out of love. When love does not rule, people suffer. I believe this; therefore, in my classroom I try to follow Christ's example and the Bible's message. I constantly strive to be kind, humble, considerate, sympathetic, patient, sincere, guileless, and generous — all ingredients of love. I also must, as I espoused earlier, be on constant guard for the log in my own eye. When you become too sure of yourself, even your own good beliefs and behaviors, you also are sure to stumble.

After reading my students' comments and thinking about the type of environment and relationships I strive to create, I've come to develop a particular metaphor: that of host. When I was growing up, I remember my mother hosting many happy parties. She frequently invited over loved ones, relatives, and family friends for holidays and summer gatherings. For each celebration, there was much preparation. Of course, we had to scrub the house down. (We were not always that neat, so these parties helped keep the house clean!) My mother also would go overboard on the food, nothing fancy, but plates of hamburgers, too many bags of buns, and an over-the-top assortment of chips and dip, apple pies, whipped cream, and ice cream. She always bought too much, a kind of family joke, so we laughed at the outrageous amounts of food piled on the party table.

Then there was the decorating and ambience. There were twinkling lights on the back porch and candles on the tables. The hot tub was steamy and beckoning. But what I remember most is my mother's joy. She so looked forward to the fellowship of the people she loved and tried to make them happy. There was never a bigger smile than the one on my mom's face greeting people at the door and embracing them with a warm hug and her deep laugh. At every gathering, there was animated and often imbibed conversation, as well as silliness, even charades. Once, when we lived on a lake, a summer party turned first into a food fight and then turned wet when everyone began to either toss people into the lake or jump in themselves. People were laughing so hard. I can still picture some guests grinning while picking seaweed and potato salad off their heads. My mother definitely knew how to throw a party. She was always a good host, putting others first and planning for their joy. At the time I didn't realize it but now I see. As the Talmud claims: Hospitality is another form of worship.

As I was thinking about this word "host," I was interested in the phrase I hear so often at church when speaking of Christ: Lord of hosts. I was intrigued. I am used to thinking in terms of a good party host, like my mother. So, what does Lord of hosts mean? Bear with me as I explain a lightbulb moment. Research reveals the following: in the Old Testament, "Lord of hosts" can be found some 200 times and more. Of course Lord means ruler or master, but who are the hosts? Various definitions reveal hosts to mean "to mass an army or servants ... ready for battle." In Exodus 12:40-41 it says:

The time that the Israelites had lived in Egypt was four hundred thirty years. At the end of four hundred thirty years, on that very day, all the companies [hosts] of the Lord went out from the land of Egypt.
— Exodus 12:40-41

In this context, it seems that the hosts are the followers of Christ who seek to serve him. In another passage, Joshua sees a man standing over him with a sword in his hand.

Joshus went to him and said to him, "Are you one of us, or one of our adversaries?" He replied, "Neither; but as commander of the army [host] of the Lord I have now come." — Joshua 5:13-14a

Today, the most common definition of "host" is my earlier description: "a person who invites guests to a social event and is *responsible* for them while they are there." I think both of these definitions are intriguing because they show the duties of one who follows Christ: to be a servant to God but also to God's people. The man with the sword says he is a commander in the Lord's army and "I have now come." He is going out among the people as both servant to his master and his master's people.

After pondering this, the lightbulb finally went off. This is how I perceive my role in the classroom. I am serving God as I serve his people. Like my mother, I strive to be a joyful host to people I love, my students, and as I do, I serve God.

Following are some of the methods I use to be a good host and spread love in the classroom. Again, whether you are a teacher or some other type of leader, I believe my methods can be used to love people in a variety of situations. As I describe these methods, visualize how they might be compared with a host warmly welcoming guests and communicating to them the message, "You are special and valuable. I love you, and I am glad you are here." This initial message, followed by a consistently godly and loving environment, has the power to create miracles in the classroom.

First Impressions

Every time you smile at someone, it is an action of love,
a gift to that person, a beautiful thing.
— Mother Teresa

The shortest distance between two people is a smile.
— author unknown

Let's get down to specifics. What do I do to make students feel singularly known and loved? Much of what I am about to share may seem simple or obvious. Yet, I believe that seemingly small, daily gestures can accomplish great results. I've also learned that what might seem obvious to me does not appear on everyone else's radar. Finally, I've found that all the warm fuzzies many of us received in kindergarten through elementary school — the lollipops, the smiley-face stickers, the hugs — seemingly turn cold by the time we turn twelve. Care and kindness, it so often turns out, is reserved only for the young.

I've tried to change that. On the very first day of class, I do a few things to let students know right away that the class will be a compassionate, empathetic, loving environment, one in which they will be uniquely valued. First, and it sounds simple, I smile warmly at every single person who enters my class on that first day. Don't underestimate the power of a smile. Mother Teresa even spoke of the importance of smiling:

> *Smile at each other, smile at your wife, smile at your*
> *husband, smile at your children, smile at each other —*
> *it doesn't matter who it is — and that will help you to*
> *grow up in greater love for each other.*[1]

My grandmother, Dorothy, who for me was as saintly as anyone I've known, always smiled. When I think of her, all I can see is her kind eyes lined by gentle wrinkles of age and her loving, embracing smile. The memory instantly makes me happy. My former college professor, Carrie Johnson, was a smiler. So were Mr. Miller and Mr. Cupal. I think their smiles conveyed an inner spirit of love that allowed them, even compelled them, to love their students. Smile often at your students and let them know you plan on loving them.

Then, after welcoming students with a smile, I go over and shake each student's hand, looking at them in the eyes while I introduce myself. "Hi, I'm Wendy Byard. Welcome to class. What is your name? Hey, I like that dog on your T-shirt. Is that a Boston Terrier? I've got one at home! Does yours like to burrow under the covers? Mine, too!"

Even at that first meeting, I try to quickly find out something about them. Do they like English? Are they from our town? What do they think about the day's weather? Right away I am letting them know that who they are and what they think is important to me. I'm also showing that we are equals, that they can talk to me and not be afraid. In Hebrews 13:2-3, it tells us: "Do not neglect to show hospitality to strangers, for by doing that some have entertained angels without knowing it." Some may be angels, but *all* are children of God.

Consider these words written to me by a student:

> It's the first day of school and my feet drag as I pull myself through the school doors toward my class. It's 9 a.m. on Monday morning, and I can think of a hundred places that I would rather be than school. I walk into my English class and find a seat at the front of the class. "Hello, I'm Wendy," a bright-eyed, bubbling blonde greets me just as I sink into my seat. She extends her hand out to shake mine ... Is this my teacher? In this moment I realize I'm not sleeping through this class.

This student's sentiments reveal the power of first impressions, that a teacher is saying right from the start that he or she cares about the individuals who walk in the door.

Later on during that first class period, while the class is working on an activity, I make it a point to learn everyone's names. I want the students to know that they are the most important aspect of the class — not the books, not my lesson plans — *them*. To accomplish this, I give the students an activity while I concentrate on learning their names. Usually, by halfway through the class period I have their names almost memorized. I think this is important. In John 10, Christ used the metaphor of the shepherd and his flock to reveal the importance, among other things, of being *known*. "I am the good shepherd, I know my own and my own know me just as the Father knows me and I know the Father" (John 10:14-15). The psalmist also declares, "O Lord, you have searched me and known me. You know when I sit down and when I rise up; you discern my thoughts from far away.... For it was you who formed my inward parts" (Psalm 139:1-2, 13).

I believe every human being craves to be known and loved singularly. Said one of my students: "I like how you try to get to know your students. Most college teachers barely even know your name. You take the time to learn about each student, and I think that's why your class is so enjoyable." So, make it your goal to know and love each student singularly and pursue an intimate relationship with every person, every gift God has put in your charge. While you're doing it, don't forget the smile! As this student reminded me, smiles matter. "I felt I could relate and be more comfortable with you more than any of my other teachers because you always had a smile on your face."

---

1. Although this has no definitive source, it has been widely attributed to Mother Teresa.

Roots: Not Just A Television Movie

Once I have welcomed students into a loving classroom, I begin the process of putting down relationship roots or laying the foundation of our relationships. To this end, during that first class period I have the students write letters to me. I encourage them to share any information that might help me to teach them more effectively or to tell me anything they want me to know about themselves.

Some students write of their dyslexia, their fears about writing, or even their pet iguanas. A few letters are deeply serious, others silly. While the class is working on an activity, I read their letters. I am quickly getting to know each student — his or her anxieties, personality, and family life.

I take these letters home and study them more closely, writing friendly and affirming notes on each letter. My comments might look like, "Don't worry, Mark, I'll help you with that." "Welcome to class, Julie! I'm excited that you love creative writing. It sounds like you have talent!"

Sometimes, I receive letters that are so painful. Just this semester, a young lady wrote of the hard experiences of her life. When I first observed Melanie, her face was drawn and tight. Her eyes darted anxiously. She impulsively blurted out comments like, "I can't do this" or "How am I going to learn this?" Melanie had been kicked out of an alternative high school and was now suffering from several personal problems. On her letter, I took special care. On the back of it, I wrote a personal letter to her. I told her to have faith in herself and her journey, that, like my dad always says when referring to a hardship, "This too shall pass." The next class period I returned the students' letters, working toward beginning our individual relationships. However, before class I returned Melanie's letter personally.

Melanie,

I just wanted you to know that I read your letter and have been thinking a lot about you. Even though you've been through many tough times, I believe you will succeed. I wrote you back a letter with some of my thoughts. Please know that I will help you in any way I can.

Wendy

She read the letter, and throughout the class I noticed a slight change in her demeanor. She seemed to smile more, to relax, and to be more engaged. Her anxious and impulsive utterances mostly stopped. When I looked at her, I made sure to smile warmly. I was letting Melanie know that in this class she was valued and cared for. As the days went by, I continued to reach out to Melanie. Yes, I witnessed a classroom miracle. I saw before me a young woman who was once full of doubt, anger, and anxiety begin to believe in herself and her abilities. Melanie began to transform, becoming aware of her many talents and, most importantly, her worth.

To me, the power of love in the classroom is so obvious, and an activity like a simple letter, the beginnings of a dialogue, can let students know you care.

One day, I collected the letters and had a doubting moment. "Do students really care about what I write on their letters? Do my little affirming comments really matter?" I was tempted to not return them and just keep the letters for myself. Then, as I was leaving class the beginning of one new semester, a bright, engaging eighteen-year-old said, "Wendy, why didn't you have our letters for us today?! I want to read your comments to us!" So, I offered up an excuse and promised to return them the following week, complete with my various thoughts and questions. I continue to believe that exchanges of intimacy and affirmation begin to spark a relationship in the classroom and create a conduit through which love can flow.

Unfortunately, from many of those letters, I perceive how many of my students suffer various fears: fear of writing, fear of presenting, fear of failure, fear of something new. Thus, I have them do some writing at the beginning of the class. One reason is to loosen up and develop their writing abilities, but mostly it is to encourage them to also value and love themselves just as God does. One day, the writing prompt was an excerpt from Marianne Williamson's book, *A Return to Love: Reflections on the Principles of a Course in Miracles*:

> *Our deepest fear is not that we are inadequate. Our deepest fear is that we are powerful beyond measure. It is our light, not our darkness, that most frightens us. We ask ourselves, "Who am I to be brilliant, gorgeous, talented, fabulous?" Actually, who are you not to be? You are a child of God. Your playing small doesn't serve the world. There's nothing enlightened about shrinking so that other people won't feel insecure around you. We are all meant to shine, as children do. We were born to make manifest the glory of God that is within us. It's not just in some of us; it's in everyone. And as we let our own light shine, we unconsciously give other people permission to do the same. As we're liberated from our own fear, our presence automatically liberates others.*[1]

Later, when that class was over, I stood by the door and thanked each student for coming, addressing each by name. I want it to be very clear to each person that he or she is singularly important to me. I care to know each one of them. Some of them are shocked that I even care to know their names. Others seem amazed that I could learn all their names or even want to. Still others warily regard it as some type of parlor trick, a fleeting means for the instructor to show off. Yet, over time and with effort, I gain their trust and build their belief that they are in a loving, validating, and empowering environment. And no, I don't forget their names.

By the second class, I use humor, perhaps even some silliness, as I call people by name and greet them as they enter the door. "Good morning, Chris, I see you've returned. What are you thinking?" By this point, I also know quite a bit about each person from reading their letters. For the remainder of the course, I get to class early, even if it's only five minutes in some cases, so I can chat with students about some of the topics they wrote about. I continue to make sure to smile at students, perhaps patting them on the back as they enter. I want them to feel welcome when they come into the room. I think this time is quite important because it creates a loving environment in which relationships can develop.

As I said, during this brief time I take what I've already learned to learn even more about them. I ask a lot of questions and also try to reveal some information about myself. In this give-and-take time, I'm creating a dynamic that has us on equal footing, so we can have a respectful, open, and caring relationship.

For example, one of my students, John, always wears his UM hat to class. I have to be well prepared on how the Wolverines' football team fared over the weekend. I often ask him if he saw the game. We would usually end up chatting about some play with several other students joining in. (It helps that I'm married to a huge sports fan!) With this early, lighthearted dialogue, I'm building relationships. It takes time, but it is well worth it. Some relationships begin with this easygoing chitchat but evolve into a classroom miracle. Such was the case with Chris.

When I met this older student, Chris was just beginning college. In fact, my course was her first college class. Right away, she began to express her nervousness. In a letter she told me, "The first day I was so scared that when I got your syllabus I nearly dropped the class. Not that it was too difficult (although I only had one class), but that I didn't have a clue what I was doing."

Over and over, throughout our beginning-of-class conversations (Chris always came in early), I tried to build her confidence. Then I began to read Chris' essays. She revealed that when she was little, her father always put her down. He told her she was worthless and could do nothing right. Those ugly seeds her father had sewn years ago took a deep and hurtful hold in Chris' life. It would take a lot to transform Chris' opinion of herself and her abilities.

On her essays I took great care to communicate what her writings meant to me, the talent they revealed, and some questions and thoughts for her to consider. Truly, through our conversations both face-to-face and through her papers, I began to see Chris' belief in herself. In fact, one day she told me she had decided to enter an

90

essay in a writing contest. Later, she would bring me an essay she wrote on her own, outside of class, that powerfully spoke of the physical abuse she and her sisters suffered at their father's hands. She wanted to teach others about the impact of abuse.

Clearly, Chris was becoming empowered. At the end of the semester, she wrote this to me: "I would like to thank you for supporting my weak self-confidence during this semester ... You made me feel confident. And for that I can't thank you enough." Then later, she wrote me this:

> *I am a fifty-year-old woman; I started in college ... after thirty years in a factory ... Arriving on campus the first day I was terrified, wondering if I was capable of achieving my educational objective. Sitting in the front row, I was greeted with a bright smile from Wendy Byard. Her friendly, caring, lighthearted teaching style soon had me calm and ready to learn. Wendy's attitude and willingness to help inspired me to overcome my reservations and excel in her class. I am very grateful that she was my first college instructor. She gave me confidence to continue on with my college education.*

Maybe you don't believe that witnessing another human being beginning to throw off chains is a miracle. Truly, what impact on the world can the changed heart of one human being have? What will be the impact of Chris' changed thinking and feeling on her husband? Her son? Her friends and neighbors? Just what good can Chris accomplish with a newfound belief in herself? Yes, I've seen kindness, an element of love, when exercised consistently, turn a teacher into a trusted mentor and begin to spark miracles in students' lives. So do what you must to show love to your students.

Doc Childre and Sara Paddison, in the *HeartMath Discovery Program*, say, "Love is not automatic. It takes conscious practice and awareness, just like playing the piano or golf. However, you have ample opportunities to practice. Everyone you meet can be your practice session."

So practice, practice, practice! It's the same advice you'd give your students, right? Consider my methods for love in the classroom and develop some of your own. Then practice them. That's the wonderful thing: You can always get better at love!

---

1. Marianne Williamson, *A Return to Love: Reflections on the Principles of a Course in Miracles* (New York: HarperCollins, 1996).

Is Your Tank Full Or Empty?

Are you happy? Do you feel loved? When you encounter others, do you feel joy? Are you excited to be with God's people? If not, how can you spread love? In other words, if you are a leader and your love tank is empty or running on low, just how is everyone around you supposed to function on high? Don't you realize that your inner well-being, your love for yourself, and your happiness is necessary to loving others? If you are unhappy, suffering, and maladjusted, you cannot serve your students well. You owe it to yourself and to them to heal and grow. Consider the words of my students. They let me know that a happy, loving, and caring teacher is very important to them.

- You inspired me the very first day of class. You stood up front cheerful, energetic, and obviously excited to teach everyone.

- It was really nice to have such an enthusiastic and passionate teacher (they seem hard to find).

- I personally enjoyed coming to class and listening to your lectures because of how upbeat you were ... whenever we as a class came in sleepy or drug down from the week, your spunky attitude lifted us up.

- It has been fun to see your energy in teaching. I can really tell that you love what you are doing. To pass your knowledge on to us as we learn.

- You ... are an inspiration for so many people as well as myself. Every day you had so much energy. I wish I could do that. You must be very happy.

- Thanks for being so positive and illuminating every morning. It's a good way to get started!

- You are by far the most enthusiastic teacher I have ever had. You are full of fun and love for teaching any student.

- Professor Byard came to class each day excited to teach us and excited to learn from us. She truly seemed to enjoy each presentation, each comment, even the little expressions her students would give off in reaction to what she was teaching us.

- You kept me on the tip of my toes the whole hour and 25 minutes.

- When I first walked into your classroom I didn't know what to expect from you, your high-energy approach to everything seemed overwhelming at first. But with time I came to realize that your enthusiasm to teach brought out my enthusiasm to learn.

- [Mrs. Byard's] teaching methods are anything but drab. She is always upbeat and shows great enthusiasm for teaching. Her delight inspires all her students to want to learn. She's so excited about her lessons that you're drawn in.

- I think you've succeeded in "teaching like your hair's on fire" as I've never had an instructor with as much enthusiasm as you!

From my students' writings, it might seem like something is seriously wrong with me! Or perhaps that I'm on some kind of stimulant! (I do like my morning coffee.) Even I am a bit shocked at how much my enthusiasm and energy registers with students. Yet, I shouldn't be. I make a conscious effort to give each class the best of me. I think this starts long before you enter the room. As

94

one of my students commented: "You must be very happy." And I am. No, I do not have a perfect life. No one does. However, I believe that to be your loving best in the classroom you must strive in your personal life for health and happiness, physically and emotionally, as well as spiritually, living and spreading the joy that is found in following Christ. In John 15, Christ said:

> *"I am the vine, you are the branches. Those who abide in me and I in them bear much fruit, because apart from me you can do nothing.... If you abide in me, and my words abide in you, ask for whatever you wish, and it will be done for you.... If you keep my commandments, you will abide in my love, just as I have kept my Father's commandments and abide in his love. I have said these things to you so that my joy may be in you, and that your joy may be complete. This is my commandment, that you love one another as I have loved you."*
> — John 15:5, 7, 10-12

Simply put, if you love God, allow his Holy Spirit in, and strive to live by Christ's example, then you will experience more joy. Then, you will have more joy to give others. I know this from my own life and what I have witnessed and read about. Spreading joy is incredibly important, as its effect can be profound as it impacts people and then reverberates outward. Henry Wadsworth Longfellow observed: "Give what you have. To someone, it may be better than you dare to think." Just think how much you could give others if you were truly joyful?

When looking back to some of the teachers you have had, do you remember those who seemed bored, condescending, disinterested, or unhappy? Were there some who rarely looked at you? Others who kept their back to you as you entered the room? Perhaps you had some teachers who never learned your name or didn't seem to care to. Where is the joy Christ spoke of? How can teachers spread joy and love to their students if it does not exist within their own souls? How can they spread joy and love if their students' happiness is not important to them?

Furthermore, I believe students are constantly looking at teachers for clues on how to live. You may think that you are only teaching algebraic equations or the Pythagorean theorem. However, students are consciously or unconsciously studying you. You are the person in authority. Your education, experience, and supposed wisdom have put these students in your charge. Thus, they must view you as a role model until their experiences with you show them otherwise. Ralph Waldo Emerson said, "Who you are speaks so loudly I can't hear what you're saying."

What are you speaking loudly? A model of love — one of patience, kindness, generosity, humility, courtesy, unselfishness, good temper, guilelessness, and sincerity? Do you have these qualities, this love in you? Is, as Christ hoped for you, "your joy complete"? If not, what will you do? Christ said there is no greater love than to lay down one's life for his friends. These words illuminate that sacrifice and service is essential to love.

Therefore, to truly love your students, you must sacrifice your negative or self-centered tendencies and beliefs. Starting today, strive to create a new inner you. Have the will to change so that your students will encounter a loving role model, one who truly shows them how to live a joyful life. Do what you must to get on the road to joy. Act! For yourself and for others. George Bernard Shaw put it so well:

> *This is the true joy of life, the being used up for a purpose recognized by yourself as a mighty one; being a force of nature instead of a feverish, selfish little clot of ailments and grievances, complaining that the world will not devote itself to making you happy. I am of the opinion that my life belongs to the community, and as long as I live, it is my privilege to do for it what I can.*[1]

---

1. George Bernard Shaw's play, *Man and Superman*, 1903. This is not copyrighted.

Love Lesson #7

God Wants Us To Have Fun

Put yourself in your students' shoes. Imagine yourself seated in your own classroom, feet firmly planted, elbows on desk, face squarely forward. Now, how do you feel? Are you enjoying yourself? Smiling? Listening intently? Maybe leaning forward to grasp some compelling point? How is the teacher behaving? Picture his or her face and body language. Recall the tone of his or her voice. Is the teacher friendly, enthusiastic, and engaging? Or do you find yourself bored, disconnected, overwhelmed, or talked down to? In other words: Would you want to be a student in your own class? If the answer is, "No," or you have to think about it, then maybe it's time for a new perspective and an overhaul of how you do things.

Why does education have to be so deadly boring or such serious business that students either sit there looking like deer caught in the headlights or victims of narcolepsy? God does not want that for us or our students. In Ecclesiastes, we are taught that God not only wants us to be winsome, he commands it: "So I commend enjoyment, for there is nothing better for people under the sun than to eat, and drink, and enjoy themselves" (Ecclesiastes 8:15a). I agree, because of course there is no better thing than to be filled with joy, regardless of the place or circumstance.

Two of my students commented on how I made the classroom fun for them.

- I liked how you made the class fun all the time. I was never bored. I always had something to do or think about. There was never a time in your class when I was not thinking. I had fun writing all the papers because they all had to do with something that has happened in my life. And I had to think back on them, and I realized some things.

- I also feel that you make writing fun. You can always make the class laugh, even when it's 9 a.m.

How do you make learning fun? How do you get students laughing, even when the sun has barely risen or you see it beginning to set through your classroom window?

It goes back to ideas I've mentioned earlier; you begin by being a good host. Greet people as they walk in the door. Ask questions. Share an interesting story about something you saw on the news. Most of my students watch *American Idol*, so as they enter they might overhear me chatting with someone about a great contestant or silly song. I then try to get others involved. I want people to feel relaxed, trusting, and part of the class community. A student wrote to me, "You inspired me. The very first day of class you stood up front cheerful, energetic, and obviously excited to teach everyone."

Also, as students enter, they'll see on the board, "Welcome!" or "It's Friday! Yeah!" These are just fun little notes to bring a smile or chuckle. In addition, I may begin the class with a story, joke, or an internet cartoon that relates to the lesson I'm about to teach. Humor conveys an important message to students: It's good and right to have fun learning.

Another way to create a more joyful environment is to always involve the students by providing interesting activities that allow them to participate. For example, during one class period we talk about people's differing perceptions of America. We read "America" by Langston Hughes and Elie Wiesel's essay "The America I Love," two different portraits of the same nation. I then ask the students to write to an imaginary person in a foreign land. This is to be a person who either knows little of America or has only been exposed to particular views. To spice it up a bit, I have the male students write to a beautiful woman named Ursula and the females write to the strapping Iglesias. In their letters, the students are to paint their own portraits of America. Then we share the letters by reading many out loud.

Some are silly, others jaded, still others touchingly patriotic. Clearly, many students are shocked by their classmates' views; quite often a spirited discussion follows. Perhaps you are saying, "That's fine for you. You're an English teacher. Just how am I supposed to involve my students and make them excited about the French Revolution?" Well, that is your job, right? Therefore, put yourself in their shoes — their age, their interests, and their level of knowledge. What will they relate to and be passionate about? What can you come up with? Be inventive! Remember, to love is to be kind. So, be kind to your students. Don't give them bland, lifeless lessons. Don't continually lecture at them or stick them will dull handouts or activities. If you don't know what else to do, seek help. Talk to fellow teachers, pick up an idea book, browse the internet, or even ask the students! Students often have great ideas. Although it may be easier and safer to stick with what you've been doing, loving others isn't effortless.

In this quote by German poet, Rainer Maria Rilke, you may think she is only referring to romantic love. But to truly love others in all situations, and to do what love truly requires, is hard. "For one human being to love another that is perhaps the most difficult of our tasks; the ultimate, the last test and proof; the work for which all other work is but preparation."

Some may react to my ideas with the thought that fun equals easy. I don't agree. You can be a challenging teacher and yet still conduct the business of education in an environment that allows people to feel relaxed, trusting, validated, and joyful. Recently a student told me: "Wendy, I am going to school to become a teacher. I like to study every teacher I have to learn their teaching techniques. Your ability to have a very personal approach but still (remain) stern is very effective and quite intriguing."

I believe that in a joyful environment, students will feel happier and more loved, thus they will be empowered and push themselves to excel and create miracles in their own lives. Dale Carnegie said, "People rarely succeed unless they have fun in what they are doing." So have fun! Smile! Laugh! And watch your students succeed. (Guess what? You just might have a little fun, too.)

Love Lesson #8

Humility

If you desire to be a god in your own classroom, then Love Lesson #8 is not for you. However, if you wish to create meaningful, loving relationships with students, you must build a sense of equality in the classroom that can only result from your humility. Yes, you are the teacher, but you are not better than your students. You are not more important, not more worthwhile, and not more pleasing to God.

Every Christmas, I watch one of my favorite holiday films: Charles Dickens' *A Christmas Carol* starring Patrick Stewart. There is a line that I think of often when I find myself climbing atop the pedestal of my own imagination. Scrooge, when asked to make a holiday donation to the needy, snidely advises that instead there needs to be a reduction in the "surplus population." However, his words come back to haunt him. Later in the story, the ghost of Christmas present turns to Scrooge and says, "It may be that in the sight of heaven, you are more worthless and less fit to live than millions."

This line often compels me to stop in my tracks and question: "Just who am I to declare myself more worthwhile than my students or anyone else?"

Yes, while I am the teacher and have education, experience, and ultimately authority in my classroom, never do I try to position myself as superior to my students or use my power for harm. Instead, I position myself as a fellow human being and child of God who has knowledge, experience, possibly some wisdom, and love to share. Furthermore, I do not perceive myself as the be-all and end-all of knowledge, nor do I want them to see me that way, either. Yes, I hope they will see the value of my knowledge, experience, and beliefs, but I am not a god in my classroom or anywhere. I am God's servant.

In addition, when I reveal information about myself, I also am trying to show a respect for our relationship by reciprocally divulging information. I might mention my children or the hometown Friday night football game. This kind of discussion shows that I do not view myself as superior to them but as part of the community — a neighbor, a friend, a servant. I am often reminded of the comment by one student, a bright, loving, young lady who had suffered many hardships but was well on her way to personal triumphs. She said, "The fact that I can talk to you and you don't make me feel inferior to you is, in my opinion, what makes you an excellent teacher."

Also, to show humility, or in Paul's words, "love vaunted not itself," I am careful of my body language. I know there are many books written about how our bodies express our feelings and beliefs. Therefore, I try to be mindful of what my body language communicates to students. For example, when speaking to a student about her paper, I might either sit down next to her at a table or crouch down so that I am at eye level. I am consciously trying to make students feel equal and comfortable. I also consider my body language in other ways. Do I stand at the front of the room with my hands on hips and my feet apart, like a general haughtily commanding her troops? Or do I walk around the room, smiling perhaps while touching someone's shoulder and kneeling down to help? The way we use our bodies conveys many messages. Consider how you use your body in the classroom and what you can do with it to show your students love.

During the second class of the semester, we engage in an introduction activity. The one I use (a well-known icebreaker) involves students interviewing each other and then introducing their partners to the rest of the class. I know some teachers believe this is a waste of time. I strongly disagree. This is a chance for me to show them I care about them individually and to also learn a great deal about them as I start to create an open, trusting, caring environment.

As each student is introduced, I ask him or her questions or comment on some aspect of their life. I might lean casually against a table at the front of the room while I smile and make respectful and inquisitive small talk. This puts people at ease, reveals humility, shows my sense of humor, and begins to create a trusting, warm environment. These first impressions, first activities, and first interactions must flow from sincere humility. They are crucial in developing a classroom in which students feel loved.

Saint Augustine said, "Humility is the foundation of all the other virtues, hence, in the soul in which this virtue does not exist there cannot be any other virtue except in mere appearance." Without the virtue of humility, it seems no other virtue can take root. Take a long, hard look in your mirror. What do you see? Do you see a humble servant or a golden calf?

Love Lesson #9

Care More Than Is Required

Once new relationships with my students have begun to sprout, I work toward deepening our relationship roots. As I've said, in my experience loving, trusting relationships create fertile ground for students achieving their highest potential, the unleashing of their miracles. Therefore, as my class progresses I make time for one-on-one conversations with my students. As I do so, I am often reminded of these words by Benjamin Franklin: "The heart of a fool is in his mouth, but the mouth of a wise man is in his heart."

Keeping this is mind, I approach conversations with my students from the heart. Remember some of their comments?

- I feel like you really care about your students. Most teachers never sit down and have a one-on-one conversation with their students.

- As a student one of the things I will remember about your class is the one-on-one relationship you had with us.

I recently watched a film about a schoolteacher, Ron Clark, and I read several articles about his beliefs and methods. Why were his students so successful? Because he loved them! He cared more than is required. Clark might have been employing the West Point cadet maxim, which implores: "Risk more than others think is safe. Care more than others think is wise...."

Clark did just that. The East Harlem teacher visited his students' homes and took them to a Broadway show. He even jumped rope with the students at recess and ultimately took his entire class to Disneyland!

Who does that?

A story like this begs the question: "When it comes to caring about students just what is *required*?" Like Clark, would you risk more than others think is safe? Care more than they think is wise? Would you take your class to Disneyland?

105

To show students you care, that you love them, you must go beyond what the culture seems to say is required and develop deeper relationships by various means. Football great and US Representative, Jack Kemp, said, "The power of one man or one woman doing the right thing for the right reason, and at the right time, is the greatest influence in our society."

I believe that loving students is the right thing for the right reason. Yet to love students, you need to create a connectedness. One of my students wrote: "You have a connection with the young students." Another said: "You always tried to reach each student individually." From their comments and my experiences, it is clear to me that people desire and deeply value this connection, this intimacy with other human beings. For in this state of connectedness, people feel secure and valued and thus free to achieve their highest potential.

I realize that in many classes, this deeper relationship may seem hard to achieve. Where is the time or the opportunity? But, if connectedness with students is truly a priority to you, you will find a way. Whether you are teaching science or keyboarding, try to implement methods to embrace and relate to your students.

For example, as I've suggested, have them write letters to you. Letters are a non-threatening means for you and your students to trade thoughts, feelings, and information. People will often reveal themselves in the private space of a letter. You can respond likewise, deepening your relationship and revealing yourself through well-placed comments and questions on their letters.

Also, once in a while leave a card for a student on his or her desk. For instance, recently a student of mine told me his mother was undergoing cancer surgery that day. Fortunately, the cancer was removed, and his mom seemed to be fine. One morning when he came into class, he found a personal note from me on his desk.

> *Eric,*
>   *I'm glad to hear that your mother is doing well. Please let me know if I can help in any way, even if it's just providing a listening ear.*
>   *Wendy*

Seemingly small gestures can have big impact, letting students know you care and that they are in an empathetic, loving environment.

You also can go beyond small acts by creating classroom assignments that allow students to personally express themselves and receive meaningful feedback about issues that are important to them. Try providing assignments that allow people to reveal, if they wish, aspects of their lives that they might desire communication about. As I described earlier, many of my students, as they begin to trust me, reveal troubling aspects of their lives through their papers and their conversations with me.

So, what do I do with this knowledge? Do I say to myself, "Well, I'm just an English teacher. Their problems are beyond the scope of why I was hired. I'm not required to help. I'm not a counselor." To this response I most strongly disagree! If you truly love other human beings, you must do all that you can to alleviate their suffering. Rabbi Abraham Joshua Heschel, who marched with Martin Luther King Jr. in Selma, said, "A religious man is a person who holds God and man in one thought at one time, at all times, who suffers harm done to others, whose greatest passion is compassion, whose greatest strength is love and defiance of despair." The loving person feels the pain of others and is not content to stand by.

Thus, when I encounter my students' troubles, I try to help. On a few occasions, I have secured money for them from the deacons' fund at my church. A young lady, who was living on her own and working a day job plus night job at a local bar, was having trouble coming to class because her car had broken down. The deacons gave her $150. Another student wrote and told me about being sexually abused by her father. I gave her the best advice I could, but directed her to the school counselor and local mental health agencies. I also told her about an excellent book. Throughout the semester, I continued to make myself available to her, providing hopeful, positive comments and a listening ear. At Christmastime my church gave several hundred dollars to an older student who had been laid off by the Ford Motor Company and had lost his home.

Furthermore, we can use our students' work to deepen our relationships and provide them with loving and enriching interactions. For example, when I work with my students on their essays, I take the time to meet with each student. As we consult over what they've written, I engage in meaningful conversations with them.

For example, one assignment involved writing about a particular impact their families have made on them. In other words, how have the students been shaped by their loved ones? When we discuss this topic, I do not approach my discussions with students in a shallow manner. Instead, I listen intently. I also empathize with my students' feelings. I allow myself to be touched and changed by their experiences and their words. I even share some of my own. I give them positive feedback, concentrating on what they did well and what they could do to make their expressions (and their own learning) even more effective to themselves and others.

From our interactions, I want them to know several things. The first is that I care. The second is that their personal expressions are valuable and have the power to impact others. The third is that they can learn from their past experiences and have ownership over their minds and their lives; a directed change or transformation is possible. I remember my experiences with one student who experienced transformation and empowerment in my English 101 course.

Toward the start of the fifteen-week course, Ann had a horrible experience. Driving home from work one night, her car was pulled over on a dark country road by what she thought was a police officer. It quickly became apparent, by the man beating on the car and screaming at her, that he definitely was not the police. Luckily, Ann escaped by spraying mace through the window and driving away. But after this incident, she was deeply troubled in many ways.

On several occasions we spoke about this experience, and she began to shape it into a powerful narrative essay as we continued to talk about it. Ultimately, Ann wrote not only an essay that helped her make sense of the experience but a research paper that offered advice to police as well as would-be victims. She even had her paper published in a nearby newspaper. Watching her transformation from a shaken, frightened young woman to a much stronger, more vocal advocate for victims was truly touching and inspiring.

I am not trying to take credit for her amazing journey. I do believe that my discussions with her and my loving attitude toward her helped Ann to begin transforming a negative situation and begin healing. As I said, I believe the Bible puts teachers ahead of miracles because teachers, through the Holy Spirit in the classroom, can help unleash miracles in students' lives. Following are some of my students' comments that reveal the impact of my religious beliefs and methods.

- I could tell that you were a very one-on-one teacher and that you cared about your students. You have definitely proven that throughout the entire semester on everything. No matter what the topic was about, a paper, homework, or a personal question, you really did listen to what I had to say.

- I looked forward to our conversations.

- Professor Byard came to each class excited to teach us and excited to learn from us.

- Each day was an exhilarating experience that has touched my mind in ways that I never realized, until I start to think! Then I see, even in my daily thought processes, that you have taught me more often than I was at first willing to admit to myself ... I felt like I could achieve anything.

Clearly, I do not believe in the assembly-line method of teaching. Most people would claim the same. Who wants to admit to such a negative metaphor? Yet, how many teachers really get out from behind their desk, move away from the blackboard, or give up that central spot at the podium to walk among their students, getting to know them while showing kindness, understanding, and generosity, among the other qualities of love?

I also don't believe you have to be an English teacher to exhibit this behavior and create this type of connectedness with students. Yes, talking with students about their personal essays and experiences does allow for intimacy more quickly. Yet, I believe that with time and effort any teacher can deepen relationships with students. However, this type of relationship, this connectedness, takes clear intention on the part of the teacher. If you desire to show your students love by knowing them, by valuing them uniquely, then you must include this on your course outcomes and develop methods to achieve this in the classroom. Real love does not happen by chance but by intention and effort.

Like my student who was traumatized on that dark country road, many other students suffer daily in various ways. Because there are so many needs in our students, we must be an ally, a resource for them. At the elementary school level, teachers see and experience so much suffering in their students. Some children come to school hungry, dirty, and tired. Others have parents who have little time for them or fight frequently, on the verge of divorce. When we observe our students' sufferings, we must make our love mean something and help them overcome their obstacles. Helen Keller wrote, "The world is full of suffering, it is also full of overcoming it."

Fortunately, Keller had Anne Sullivan, the teacher who, out of her sympathies for the Kellers and Helen's plight, undertook a task many said was impossible. With Sullivan's love, Keller went on to achieve a great many things, including graduating *cum laude* from Radcliffe College. French philosopher and social activist, Simone Weil, said, "The capacity to give one's attention to a sufferer is a very rare and difficult thing; it is almost a miracle; it is a miracle." Appropriately, the play and film about Keller and Sullivan's lives were titled *The Miracle Worker.*

What miracles will you help unleash in your students' lives? What transformations will be made? Will you take on the uneasy tasks? Will you go beyond what is required? Will you love them?

I also try to help my students and deepen our relationships by revealing my own struggles and offering the wisdom and hope gained with age.

Tom,

I, too was anxious when I entered the sixth grade. I was shy and only had one best friend who seemed to be ditching me for the popular girls. So, I understand how it must have felt for you. But you know what? One day I got courageous. I ran up to some girls on the playground and asked them if I could play with them. I was extremely nervous. They were sitting up high on the jungle bars staring down at me. I could have run away. But I didn't. I believed that they would like me because, frankly, I liked me and God loves me! And you know what? To this day, some thirty years later, we are still good friends! So have faith in yourself, Tom, and the world around you. And don't let past negative experiences control your future.

Wendy

You also could try writing unexpected positive notes on their work occasionally. "Outstanding effort all semester, Miranda! I'm so proud of your work ethic." Or, "Jim, that was a thoughtful comment you made during Tuesday's discussion. It opened my eyes to a different view. Thank you." Affirmations such as these will have a strong impact on students' feelings of worth.

Think back to the kind words you have heard in your lifetime. Do you remember who said them and where you were when you heard them? I bet you do. Positive words are like unexpected presents. I think we remember them always and are changed by them immeasurably. Recently I helped plan a fiftieth wedding anniversary party for my in-laws. I put a lot of work into every detail. The night of the party, my husband's uncle turned to me and said, "You know, Wendy, you're great." Wow. I was really touched. When was the last time someone told you were great? For most of us, probably never. I can't recall ever being told I was great. Affirming comments like that might stick with us forever, validating and uplifting us.

Tell your students they are great. Take them aside once in a while or write them a note and tell them about some special quality they possess or exemplary effort they have displayed. They might remember it for the rest of their lives. I am reminded of my daughter, Kacie. A few years ago, a teacher had an activity that involved each of her students one at a time. On a given day, she had every student in her class write something positive about one particular student. On the day it was my daughter's turn, she rushed home to show me all the kind comments the boys and girls had written. Do you think she threw those comments away? No, they are tucked away with my daughter's special keepsakes. Praise is so rare and so necessary; we should give it more freely and more often.

At the end of the semester, the very last day of class, my students come in to pick up their research papers and say good-bye. In many classes, the end of the semester or school year means simply walking away with a final test in hand or a bundle of papers in tow. Oftentimes, a student and teacher never even say good-bye. The class just ends and both parties quietly slip away. Yet, why not have this time be an opportunity to let students know how much you truly care and admire them for their unique gifts?

On the last day of my classes, I bring in treats. One semester, at Christmastime I brought in a pot of steaming cocoa with sprinkles and an assortment of decorated cookies. Harry Connick holiday songs drifted throughout the classroom. I even brought in a twinkling little Christmas tree (although slightly crooked) my young daughter had made in preschool. The atmosphere was warm and festive.

As my students begin entering the room to pick up their papers and drop off their letters to me, I make a clear point to let them know how wonderful I think they are. I shake hands, and I give hugs. I also sing their praises: "Brandon, you are such a fine young man. I was privileged to be your teacher this semester. I always appreciated the thoughtful comments you made in class and the depth of thinking in your papers. For example, your essay 'Liberty's Steel' allowed me to see a deeper meaning behind America's great projects. So, thank you, Brandon!"

Then, before students leave, I also make a point of letting them know that they can contact me at any time for help, advice, and reference letters. Just because the class ends, our relationship doesn't have to end. I also continue to pray for them as I think of them often.

It is important not to wait until the end of the class to start developing deeper relationships. All throughout, make an effort to get to know students on a more intimate level so that your final good-byes truly do represent a meaningful transition. As I mentioned earlier, you can build your relationships with students and let them know you care by consistently asking them questions about themselves and engaging in thoughtful conversations. Take an interest in the unique aspects of their lives.

"Mark, how did your piano recital go Thursday?" Or, "Heidi, how is your son's asthma? Is he doing any better? Did you read that recent article about new treatments?" What I'm saying is to make a point to learn about your students' lives and unique interests and develop a real relationship with them. To this end, visit them at lunch or recess from time to time. At the community college where I teach, I make a point before and after class to go out among the tables where students gather. I'll stop and visit with a student for a while or sit down amongst a table of current or past students.

In addition, I'll even call them at home once in a while. "Lori, this is your teacher, Wendy. I just wanted to let you know that I'm really proud of you and how your paper turned out. You worked hard, and it shows. Great job! I'll see you tomorrow." Calling a student at home for nothing but positive comments will come as a total shock, trust me. It most assuredly will make him or her feel good, cared for, and motivated to do even better. In this loving environment, most students blossom.

In addition to positive words, another idea I'll share with you is the "home-run handshake." Ever hit a home run? Unfortunately, I haven't. The closest I've come is watching them on television. As a Detroit sports fan, on many occasions one spring I watched Tigers hitter, Chris Shelton, pound a home run into the bleachers. After rounding the bases, Chris would happily run into the dugout where he was congratulated by slaps on the back and hearty handshakes. Oh, the feeling of accomplishment and the recognition of a job well done! Most of us will never be major league power hitters, but that doesn't mean we can't be congratulated for our efforts and achievements.

Therefore, and it might sound a little strange at first, as I collect every major writing assignment, I give each student a sincere and enthusiastic handshake. In other words, I take their papers, shake their hands, and make a few glowing comments. "Congratulations! You got it done!" "Nice effort! I know it wasn't easy, Mike, but you did it. Good for you!" The first time I shake my students' hands, I receive many interesting responses. Some laugh, others shake their heads and smile, some really get into it, pumping my hand with gusto, while many just seem plain shocked. Yet, all seem to like it. It's not very often that people are affirmed for their efforts.

When was the last time someone told you, "Good job!"? So, as corny as it might seem to some, I continue to engage in the home-run handshake. Recently, I decided to ask a few of my students what it meant to them. Maybe I was wrong, I wondered. Maybe I overestimated the meaning of my handshakes. Maybe it is too corny.

I approached Erica and Kathy, and asked, "Ladies, when I shake your hands in class, what does it really mean to both of you?" Their responses were similar and sincere: "I feel you care about us. It's like you are trying to have a connection with us. You look us right in the eye, smile at us, and touch us. When you are doing that, I feel I have a closer relationship with you and that you care." In a letter I received, one student wrote these words:

- Mrs. Byard also shows a zest for her students. Whenever I would turn in a paper, Wendy would shake my hand. This little gesture meant a lot to me as a student. She was acknowledging that I had worked hard on this paper and that it meant something.

I know what a few of you might be thinking: "Why should I give my students a handshake for a simple paper or project being turned in? Not every essay is a home run." Well, even stepping up to the plate, swinging the bat, and making contact with the ball is a worthy effort. Maybe as teachers we've forgotten how difficult classwork can be and how often it is demoralizing or unheralded. I think the effort deserves recognition. I also believe that praise inspires. When you tell someone you appreciate his efforts and are proud of his achievements, in fact he or she feels inspired and motivated to improve. They understand that they've come in contact with a person who cares about their effort and success. Thus, students may be galvanized to reach even higher heights. Even though it might feel a little awkward at first, consider using the home-run handshake in your classroom. Praise can make your students feel like power hitters, maybe perform like them, too.

Another idea to consider is sitting down with your students and discussing assignments with them one-on-one in a relaxed manner. Sit down at a round table or next to each other to also give the feeling of equality. Approach it as a consultant: Be positive and use a give-and-take style. Ask questions and really listen. Smile a lot. Remember Mother Teresa's comments about the effect of a smile. Radiate warmth. Give a touch on the shoulder once in a while.

I know some of you are saying, "Whoa, Wendy, in this day and age I wouldn't touch my students anywhere. I might get sued for sexual harassment!" Like Jack Kemp, I believe in doing what is right, not kowtowing to fear. So, I will continue to provide my students with warmth and affection. Psychotherapist Carmelia Elliot said, "Make yourself a blessing to someone. Your kind smile or pat on the back just might pull someone back from the edge."

In addition to some of the above ideas, I believe teachers, when discussing student assignments, should speak to their students in a respectful and kind manner. Not long ago, some of the secretaries at the community college where I teach were speaking about an instructor who supposedly yells at her students. It seems possible as I have heard her disparaging remarks in the staff lounge. I believe this is completely unacceptable. If you have divined, as I have, that students are wonderful creations of God, then how can anyone justify the humiliating and unkind treatment of them?

Teachers have been placed before miracles in the Bible. It seems clear that God gives them this important placement for a reason: to help create miracles in people's lives. I just don't believe this is possible while you are screaming at people and disparaging them to others.

Examine your beliefs and the actions that flow from them. Are you an uplifting force in the classroom? Are you a loving force? Do you follow the Golden Rule, treating your students as you would be treated and loving your students as you are loved? Are you the teacher God spoke of, the teacher he placed before miracles? Would he be pleased with your treatment of his people?

Love Lesson #10

Love Me Tender
(And Sometimes Tough)

Surprisingly to some, the Golden Rule is not just about warm fuzzies. Yes, we are commanded to love our neighbor as ourselves. Usually, the way we want to be loved is by chocolates, candlelight, and bubble baths. No one really wants the other side of the coin: tough love. No, we really don't want to be held responsible for our poor decisions; no, we don't want to hear what we've done wrong; no, we don't want to know what we could do better. To many, tough love stinks. It's hard. Just give me a lollipop and let me be on my way.

However, I do believe that the Golden Rule calls for a certain amount of teacherly toughness. Ironically though it might seem, I think tough love falls under kindness. One of Paul's love ingredients for toughness, combined with tenderness, is kindness. A tough but tender act, done for the benefit of another, is most definitely undertaken in his or her best interest.

Therefore, in my classroom I can be tough. I have high standards and expectations. Yes, I give out candy once in a while, but I also give out a dose of tough medicine when the situation calls for it. Tough love is necessary for self-reflection, self-awareness, and growth. Yes, tough love can be hard. But it is still love. This tension reveals itself immediately on the first day of my class.

"What do you mean you're taking attendance? This is a college class. I'm an adult. It should be up to me whether I come to class or not."

This is a type of statement I hear occasionally from those who are bold enough to speak out that first day of class or soon after.

"Mr. Smith, my psychology teacher, doesn't take attendance. Why should you?"

"Well," I reply, "out of a class of thirty, how many students regularly come to Mr. Smith's class?"

"Uh, maybe twelve."

"And of that twelve, how many stay for the entire 85-minute period?"

"I usually stay. Sometimes Mark stays. Oh, and the twins stay."

"So, out of thirty students, only four students are learning the full amount of what Mr. Smith has to offer. That's not too many, is it?"

"No, I guess not," says my student reluctantly.

And I continue. "You also seem to be claiming that not caring whether students come to class and being indifferent to whether students stay through the class is a good thing. I strongly disagree. I care about you. Thus, I care about you getting the most out of my class. This may be your one opportunity in life to grasp a particular concept, learn an important fact, or gain a necessary insight. I'm going to make sure you have that chance. Therefore, yes, attendance will be taken — every day. Plan on being here."

"What if I'm not?"

"Then I'll track you down," I respond laughingly, but students know I mean it. I've called them at home several times.

This same attitude should apply to all aspects of one's teaching. We should expect students to be on time, to turn in their assignments when they are due, to listen in class, and to put in a considerable effort. When students don't, we should then step in and do whatever is in our power to help students develop in maturity, work habits, and so on. This is the Golden Rule: Do unto others as you would have done to you. Hopefully, by now most people realize that the people who love them the most expect the most. A student commented on this in a letter she wrote to me.

- Although Wendy showed appreciation for my work, she didn't let me off with an easy grade. This was a class where you earned your grade. Each paper I received back would be packed full of comments. Wendy would explain everything that I could do to improve my essay. It was nothing abnormal to have a two-page response from Wendy. After all the comments Mrs. Byard would then decide on an appropriate grade, and sometimes it wasn't as high as I would have hoped for. (Yet) each piece I write is now fascinating, grammatically correct, and passionate. Wendy has strongly affected me and my passion for English.

Yes, I do believe students need high expectations. However, I do want to add a caveat to this lesson: Tough love is not cruel. As I said earlier, kindness is toughness combined with tenderness. For example, if a student is missing class, you try to find out why and you try to help. You don't automatically assume the worst and simply write "absent" in the grade book with no further thought to the matter. Oftentimes, when I approach absent students and seek to find out why they miss class, their answers surprise and sadden me. One young lady, who was bright but seemingly dejected in class, quit coming for a week. So I called her at home.

"Elaine, why haven't you been in class? You know it's important for you to be there, and you know I expect it. Because you were absent, you didn't turn your paper in."

Her reply? "Yes, I know, Wendy, but I really couldn't come to class this week. My grandma is sick with cancer, and she lives with my dad and me. Mrs. Riley, her caretaker, came down sick, so I had to stay home with Grandma."

In this situation, I had a couple of options. I could say, cruelly, "Well, I am sorry, too, Elaine, but rules are rules. The paper was due Tuesday. I am sorry about your grandma, but I cannot accept a late paper."

Does this sound heartless? Can you believe any teacher would say this? Well, they do. Sometimes teachers will publicly declare their inflexible approaches like a badge of honor. One teacher proudly exclaimed that she never accepts a late paper, "even if the student is dead and knockin' on heaven's door."

To me, this is not tough love. That type of decision making lacks compassion and wisdom. My student did not choose for her grandmother to have cancer. She did not choose to skip class and skip my deadline. She was compelled to take care of someone she loves dearly. I am glad she made that choice to stay home. That shows far more about her character and her wisdom. Treating students with loving toughness shows much more about ours.

Now, of course, not every student who misses class is tending to a dying relative. Some skip class for a Tim Horton's donut or to watch *The Price Is Right* on television. The point is that we care enough about our students to seek them out and to communicate with them. We try to find out why they are doing what they do. Then, we try to help them improve. Yes, sometimes help comes in the form of a "no." Other times, it's a second chance, a listening ear, or some other form of help.

That sounds good. Tough but tender love, I like that. I'll do that. I'll expect more from my students and hold them accountable, all for their own good. But wait a minute. I'm not done. Your students are not the only ones who need the tough-and-tender approach. What about you? As a teacher, do you expect a great deal from yourself and hold yourself to high standards? Or, with some honest soul-searching, do you find that you need to get tough with you?

Recently, I was feeling smug and proud of myself. On a warm, breezy Friday afternoon I had subbed for a fellow teacher. Afterward, several older students approached me, thanking me for insights I had shared about writing.

"Wendy, it was so good to hear some concrete advice. I don't mean any disrespect, but this is the first year for our teacher, and it seems she still has a bit to learn. It was helpful to hear what you had to say."

I walked out of that room with an arrogant smile on my face. Good for me! I'm an accomplished teacher! But by the time I had reached home, I felt sickened by my attitude. I am not perfect. Far from it. Like any other, my sins are always with me. In fact, when I take a tough look at myself, I see definite areas needing improvement. Again, that uncomfortable passage from the Bible worms its way into my head: "Why do you see the speck in your neighbor's eye, but do not notice the log in your own eye?"

So, yes, be tough, but also be tender with your students in seeking the best for them. Also be tough (and tender) with yourself. How can you truly give your best to your students if you don't expect and demand the best from yourself?

Love Lesson #11

Watch Your Language

Students hate the red pen! Essays and research papers are returned splattered in red teacher comments until very little of the original text is even visible. Very few of us use a red pen anymore. We've opted for plain, old black or perhaps happy purple. Yet, the impact often remains the same: a crushing of the spirit. Our negative comments and derogatory words can slice people deeply.

However, loving criticism, that is, words offered with respect and kindness, can transform and inspire students.

- I did like how on the comments you put on my papers that they were very personal, yet you were still able to give your opinion about it in a good manner. I have had other English teachers just write a grade or tell me what I did wrong on my papers. In this class I really got to know what you felt and thought about my papers and what could be changed.

- I really appreciate the personalized analysis of my writings and the helpful suggestions that you offered ... I think that you are a very good judge of students and cater to their own needs very well.

- I like the way you advised us on improving our writing.

- I also enjoy your honesty and openness.

- This past semester gave me a lot of confidence not only in myself but in my writing. Your acceptance and feedback on my essays will help me in my writing for years to come. I don't think I've ever had to put as much thought into my writing as I did this semester.

- You gave me the confidence to read my paper in front of the whole class.

- I greatly appreciate the time you take to explain the class assignments and the time you take to give each individual student the attention and help they need.

- I appreciate all the extra time you spent after class. Not many teachers have patience for staying after as much as you have.

- Your class was filled with fun activities, games, and laughter. Then in grading papers you gave a down-to-earth response. The comments you made were there to help improve one's abilities, not to cut down the author.

- So when you were inspired by my papers it gave me the confidence I needed to believe in myself.

Some teachers seem to believe that focusing on pointing out flaws while using brutal honesty is the best way to go.

"We're just trying to help! Students need to know what they're doing wrong! They must understand the rules for when they venture out into the real world!"

We've probably all thought or uttered these types of justifications for marking our students' papers with comments aimed at highlighting mistakes and weaknesses. Most of us are well-intentioned. However, unfortunately, I believe there some teachers who either bury their students under a well-meaning mountain of criticism or possibly enjoy the superiority of knowing more than their students. I have overhead comments around the coffeepot that to me reveal counterproductive beliefs. I also am reminded of a recent acquaintance who told me how it was always her desire to become an English teacher.

"I love to catch people breaking grammar rules," she smiled. I think I even detected a sadistic twinkle in her eye!

A local newspaper columnist in a nearby town has devoted several columns to gleefully "catching" people breaking the "rules" of English. Readers are happily submitting examples of rule breakers, thus showcasing their knowledge and superiority over those who are seen as ignorant and in offense.

Hmm. Love is comprised of humility, kindness, and generosity. However, some teachers who always have had a particular aptitude for their subject matter, like most English teachers who are naturally adept at language, might "correct" their students with a tone that might be hurtful, condescending, or, admit it, even a bit gleeful.

Be clear as to what your motivations are. Yes, you are trying to help, but we often carry personal baggage that informs our view and treatment of others. Sometimes we have a need to impress, or we're incredulous that someone doesn't know how to use the semicolon simply because we know how to use it! Do you know what a starter solenoid is? Your mechanic probably does. How would you like it if, through his tone, he conveyed, "Sheesh, Mrs. Jones, everyone knows what the function of the starter solenoid is! What's wrong with you?" Thus, when you pick up that weighty pen, consider your motivations. What are you really trying to accomplish? Then consider Paul's words: "Rejoiceth not in iniquity," because most certainly unkindness is wickedness.

Of course, as teachers, we must teach. But a loving teacher is a kind teacher. Consider the tone of your comments. Do you remember any negative comment that was emblazoned across one of your early papers? I can still recall a comment that appeared on one of my graduate research papers. I was so excited to get that paper back; I had worked extremely hard on it. Quickly my eyes fell to his remarks: "Your comments make you seem very provincial." I read his words; at the time I wasn't even sure what provincial meant. However, it didn't seem good.

When I got home, I quickly looked it up. "Provincial: not fashionable or sophisticated." This was followed by several negative and somewhat condescending remarks. Nowhere on my paper were there any positive comments — nada — zilch. Thus, his unkind view of my work was even more of a stinging slap. If you've ever been slapped, you remember it. One of my students, in her first-day-of class letter to me, wrote, "As one of my teachers told me, 'You're the queen of bullshit.' " To this day, she has not forgotten that comment. It's funny how the hurtful words often register so much more powerfully than the loving. Perhaps it is because the kind word often goes unsaid, while the hurtful seem so plentiful and cruelly delivered.

When I comment on my students' papers, I keep that in mind. I always begin with what the paper meant to me. How or what did it make me feel, think, or believe? For example, I once had a student who wrote an essay about her husband's affair. She was "happily" married with three small children when she found out he was cheating. This student wrote an extremely honest and vulnerable paper about what she had discovered about her own self-worth. As her instructor, I did not begin with, "Sue, your paper shows a lack of coherence" or even "I really liked your organization." No, instead I began with how the work impacted me — one human being to another. I told her how I also had to grapple with issues of self-worth, not because of a cheating husband, but because of the identity issues that often accompany being a mother. I, too, have three children and have felt displaced from time to time.

What I first engaged in with my student was a conversation, a meeting of two minds. I let her know what I learned and felt from reading her work and what thoughts her words prompted in me. Her efforts were validated by my sincere and kindly worded interaction.

Then, I concentrated on what I liked, what I thought was effective in her essay. I tried to be as specific as possible. "I like the way you concluded that paragraph. Your final sentence flowed logically from your support, yet it was unexpected, too. That made it more satisfying." I think it's important people know what they've done well. This validates them. I also believe that people's efforts flow from their child within, that part of them that seeks love and acceptance. Remember Mother Teresa's quote? "There is more hunger for love and acceptance in this world than for bread"?

After commenting on the aspects of my students' work that seem worthwhile and effective, I move on to my "suggestions." I begin this way: "To improve your paper, I suggest...." By using the word "improve," I am not conveying that the paper is horrible or unworthy. Instead, I am indicating that I am a partner, helping to point out possible ways of making it even better. Also, by using the word "suggest," I am inserting respect and equality into the interaction. In the end, I must assign a grade. I grapple with this need to assign a grade or number, as I know many teachers do. I am still trying to convey that my views are not the be-all and end-all.

Yes, I would hope that my students see wisdom in my comments. However, I am not going to position myself as a god in the classroom — all-knowing. I tell them that I believe my education and experience have taught me much, and I am simply passing along what I know. Yet, they ultimately are in charge of their work and must make decisions for themselves.

I know many teachers do not adhere to this view. They believe that in their classrooms, they are the final arbiter of what is good work. However, this makes me a little nervous. As I've said and as Paul has instructed, love is humble. When the instructor exalts himself as the undisputed bearer of all knowledge, then the possibility for oppression exists, and the presence of love diminishes. The students become captive to the instructor in a variety of ways. I'll give you an example.

There is a teacher where I work who holds very firm views. When she expresses herself, it is with strong conviction as to the rightness of her opinions. Recently, she told me that in her class students are only to learn the five-paragraph essay, nothing else. Of course, many teachers agree. (I do not.) Something else she said deeply concerned me. "Students are like babies. They need their hands held. The five-paragraph essay is safe for them. In any situation, they can use it and never be confused." I tried to politely express a different point of view to her but to little avail. Unfortunately, when teachers see themselves as having all the answers, they are not open to new ways of seeing and doing, which can lead to profound consequences for students.

In my composition courses, I reveal my humility by explaining that I am not the final judge. Yes, I have experience, and I believe I have worthwhile input. However, if I assume the role of final judge, I risk blinding myself to the divine spark of unique creativity in each student. In other words, while I am demanding a five-paragraph essay in every situation, I am shutting down the special and individual talent of the student who has a different vision. Perhaps he saw a different, more creative, more compelling way to achieve the same goal. Yes, I believe in giving students the various tools they'll need to create, but at some point you have to allow the student to become the artist. Perhaps the student has the means to create a different world, one I never imagined or knew existed.

Harry Chapin's song "Flowers Are Red" so poignantly points out how teachers can use their power to destroy individuality and diminish love in the classroom. In the song, a small boy wants to paint his flowers in many different colors. But the teacher demands that the boy paint the grass green and the flowers red to replicate the natural world. The teacher says that there is no "need" for any other response. However, the child tries to resist; he has a different vision of the world. But the teacher and the system persist at crushing the boy's will and his unique perspective. The boy relents and bows down to the authority's mandate. He does as he is told: He paints his flowers red.

How does this scenario destroy love? It replaces love with selfishness. Blaise Pascal, the French philosopher, said, "Those who do not hate their own selfishness and regard themselves as more important than the rest of the world are blind because the truth lies elsewhere." One of my students responded to my beliefs and wrote this to me.

- I also have learned from you a lot in the sense that you don't always have to follow the grain in life. To do something different or make a bold move in writing a paper can sometimes be okay. The grades you get and the courses you take will come and go, but knowing that you worked hard at something and stand behind it 100% is what counts.

Again, teachers should look to Paul's instruction on love. "Love is patient ... love is not envious.... It does not insist on its own way"

(1 Corinthians 13:4-5a). Therefore, in the classroom, seek to be a servant, not a master. Serve your students by helping them unleash their miracles, the divine spark within each of them that allows for unique and special creations.

Your enslavement of your students also hurts yourself. Frederick Douglass said, "No man can put a chain about the ankle of his fellow man without at last finding the other end fastened about his own neck." When you become the know-all master in the room, chaining your students to your ideas, beliefs, and ways of doing, you similarly imprison yourself, as you are unable to experience the surprise, wonder, and joy at seeing what other human beings are capable of creating. Thus, the master, the controlling teacher, may, in the end, be the most enslaved of all as he shuts himself off to all the beautiful flowers in the garden when he chooses to focus solely on the one bloom he has consistently admired.

Just recently, I took a trip to Chicago and visited its art museum. Walking from room to room, I marveled at the individual talent and vision of each artist. So many different works of art, expressed in a variety of colors and forms!

Why should we, as teachers, have the right to suppress the God-given vision and expression of our students? Instead, we should provide the tools. We should teach them the worthwhile traditions that have been passed down to us. Five-paragraph essays do have a place, but do not claim that is all or that there is nothing of worth beyond your ways of seeing and doing! Instead, open the door for unique expression — for the Picassos, the Gertrude Steins. Realize that God has bestowed special gifts on each individual, and help each student to discover and develop them. Don't be the self-appointed god, armed with a sword of red, slashing papers with a seemingly well-intentioned but ultimately cruel or limiting result. How many students have been permanently injured by these well-meaning gods who politely but firmly demand that flowers must be red? So, get humble, stay humble, and put the red pen in storage.

Love Lesson #12

Save A Seat For The Savior

Several years ago, when my two oldest daughters were little, they came home from church one Sunday morning with vibrantly colored bands on their tiny wrists. Neon yellow, hot pink, royal blue — the powerful hues immediately drew my eye. "Girls, what beautiful bracelets," I commented. "Why were you given those today?" "Oh, Mom," they replied, eyes rolling, "don't you see the letters on them? WWJD." As I said, this was a while ago, before the phrase "What would Jesus do?" became a worldwide and instantly recognizable acronym designed to spur people into right thought and action. This was my first time being exposed to those four letters that now seem to pop into my head so often.

Maybe you're like me. Maybe some days you find yourself in troubling situations and truly wonder, "What should I do? What would Jesus do?" Hearkening that question helps to make your response clear. You know Jesus' response would be one of love, kindness, humility, generosity, or any other of the ingredients of love revealed more specifically by Paul. But on other days — on those days that you feel grouchy, rushed, overwhelmed, and frustrated — you barely think of Jesus at all, let alone wonder what he would do after being cut off on a busy highway by a speeding semi. Would Jesus curse? Would he roll down the window and gesture? Would Jesus even speed up and try to veer in front of the offending truck? Of course not. But we don't often turn to Jesus when it feels so good to be bad.

That is why I've begun a new tradition in my classroom: I save a seat for the Savior. Typically, in my English courses I have 29 students. There are always enough blue plastic and metal chairs for every student with a few left over. One day, after seeing WWJD displayed on a local poster, the idea came to me. What if I gave Jesus a prominent seat in my classroom? What if I symbolically placed a chair for him somewhere in my room to remind myself that God is always present and to turn to him in those troubling

129

moments when I feel frustrated, angry, bored, or simply unsure? Perhaps by placing a visible and constant reminder of Jesus and what his life on Earth revealed, I would be more aware of God's constant presence and inspired to follow God's ultimate lesson plan: His "will be done on Earth as it is in heaven." With such a symbol in my classroom, perhaps I would work harder to be God's representative to my students, striving to be my best self and consistently loving them in thought, word, and deed.

I was excited by my new idea, so one morning I got to class early. I was going to choose one of the new blue plastic chairs and find the perfect spot for it in the room, a place where I could see it from almost any angle. Yet, when I entered the room and turned to look around, I immediately was taken aback. There, amongst all the uniform blue chairs was a brand new chair.

I had never seen it before in the room. It was totally unlike the others. First, it was old, as if it came from some long-ago elementary school classroom. The chair's design recalled the 1950s with its boxy shape, large metal legs, and large square of faux leather for a back. But its color was what intrigued me: It was bright gold, a most unusual color for a classroom chair or any chair for that matter.

In my years of teaching at this large college building of many classrooms, I had not once seen a chair like this. Yet today, on this very day that I was making a conscious decision to save a seat for Jesus, this unique and colorful chair appeared. Was this by chance? Perhaps, however, I choose to believe that once I invited the Savior into my classroom, he provided his seat.

Now when I find an unkind thought beginning to percolate in my mind or I catch myself about to say something ungracious, I look over at the chair. I know God is in the classroom with me, guiding me, and I picture the kind and gentle teacher that Jesus was and wonder what he would do if he were me. It helps to know the ultimate teacher is in my classroom. When I seek to do his will on Earth, how can I go wrong?

Saving a seat for Jesus also sparked in me another important thought: I should begin praying to God regularly on behalf of my students. In the past, from time to time, I had prayed for a particular student. I recall a vibrant young man, blessed with wit and a crown of wavy brown hair, but also burdened with an alcoholic father. He came to me with his problems, the most immediate one was being kicked out of his often violent home by his dad. His frightened mother had begun sneaking him in through the basement window late at night so that her drunk, abusive husband would not hear their son coming home.

When I heard of this situation, I tried to counsel the young man, I tried to be a listening ear, and I referred him to other resources in the community. I also began praying for him. I asked God to help this precious person find a better living situation, so that he could pursue his education and a better life. Fortunately, it did not take long for my prayers to be answered; this young man did find a better place to live. The Bible assures us:

> *And this is the boldness we have in him, that if we ask anything according to his will, he hears us. And if we know that he hears us in whatever we ask, we know that we have obtained the requests made of him.*
> — 1 John 5:14-15

Yes, I did pray for students occasionally. When I noticed the gold chair in my room, and it truly dawned on me that God was in this place, wanting me to help create his miracles, I thought: "I should pray for each of my students on a regular basis." This might seem overwhelming and difficult, especially if you're a teacher of many classes with many students. However, I believe if your heart is willing, you will find a way — his way.

Therefore, be inventive. Perhaps every Monday morning, before the day's classes begin, sit down with a list of your students' names. Say each name out loud and then pray for them or submit the entire list of names.

Another idea I am about to try in my classroom is a Student Prayer Journal or, for a little naming fun, Prayers4Pupils. The idea is to keep a journal of all my students so I can record the various issues in their lives that seem to call out for God's assistance.

131

Last semester I had a student who was bullied throughout elementary and high school. Now, as a college student, he seemed to struggle with his identity, and he needed to fit in. I would think of Carl and his problems from time to time, maybe while I was grocery shopping or driving around town, so my thoughts were random and fleeting. Also, my thoughts weren't prayers.

However, a Student Prayer Journal makes prayer a priority and thus a planned, consistent event. When you see a need in your student's life, you write it down. You make notes, then you pray on the problem and ask God for his guidance and love. This journal should also keep you mindful of your students' needs and encourage you, with God's help, to seek solutions on their behalf.

Many of us keep "To Do" lists about seemingly important errands: buy milk, take dog to vet, vacuum living room. However, how many of us write down the much more important errands with which we should be concerned? How many of us write down about finding ways to love our students better? Pray to God and strive to endeavor daily to fulfill his ultimate lesson plan. God put you, a teacher, ahead of miracles because through you he can accomplish his loving will on Earth.

Section Three:

Conclusion

Love Now! Miracles Await!

*Our Father does not inspire us to do that which cannot
be done.*   — Saint Therese

I began this book with the miracle of Bill. Yet there are so
many miracles to come, like the ones I wish for a young man I met
in my class recently: Ryan. On that first day of class, he lazily
plopped down into a chair at the back of the room. His disinterested gaze, tousled bed hair, and wisecracking manner had me intrigued. He did everything he could to appear aloof and more clever
than the rest of us. Some teachers might have been annoyed. In
fact, Ryan told me that many of his high school teachers did get
fed up with his "attitude" and often sent him to the office or eventually ignored him. But as I said, I was compelled to know and
understand why Ryan behaved the way he did. Then I read his first
essay.

His paper revealed a difficult childhood with a neglectful, abusive mother. In it, he even referred to her as a "Nazi." I also recall
another painful moment that followed Easter weekend. Before class,
I asked some of the students a bit jokingly (being that they were
young adults) if they had received any Easter baskets from the
Easter Bunny, meaning their parents. Several students enthusiastically told me, "Yes!" Many had awakened Easter morning to baskets filled with candy, CDs, iTunes gift cards, and gum. Suddenly,
Ryan remarked pointedly to the entire group: "I never got an Easter basket, not even when I was a little kid."

An uncomfortable silence followed, while we all tried to discern the meaning and pain behind his words. Later in the semester,
Ryan also would tell the class that the police were common visi-
tors at his volatile childhood home. After hearing his various comments, I asked him once if he had been physically abused as a
child. Ryan wouldn't answer me, but he smirked tellingly, staring
me in the eyes, his dark unblinking eyes revealing all. In time, I
came to understand that his joking, smirking manner was a defen-
sive mechanism, a means of coping with what must have been a
cruel and painful upbringing.

At the beginning of my class, Ryan often showed up late. He'd saunter in, slouch down in his chair, throw his arm lazily across the adjacent chair, and spend much of the hour talking and making jokes with a classmate. I admit, I did get somewhat irritated, but I made it my mission, as I do with all my students, to love him and let him know it. After I received his essay, the one revealing a hard upbringing and poor relationship with his mother, I began talking to him more intimately. I asked questions. I listened. I joked with him. I inquired about his job at a local store. I also began building him up. I told Ryan how bright he was. To me, comedians are almost always highly intelligent people. Ryan's quick wit and humorous observations, although often cynical, were the marks of a keen mind. I reminded him of that constantly, both on his papers and when we talked both in and out of class.

"Ryan," I would tell him, "you have so many gifts, so many talents. I just wish the best for you. I know one day I'll run into you on the street and see such a successful person. And why not? You have all you need for a wonderful life."

One day, I even talked to him about my own father and his alcoholic parents who made for a disturbing and painful upbringing. I explained some parallels I saw between my dad and Ryan and how I did not want him to suffer like my father had suffered throughout his life with negative feelings and ugly images. For Ryan, I wanted a happy life, and I implored him to make his own healing and joy a priority. Through smirks and jokes, I think Ryan began to listen. I then started to notice something interesting. Ryan began showing up early for my class.

"Well, Mr. Turner, you're here early today. To what do I owe this distinct pleasure?" (Sometimes, I'd slip into this silly demeanor and tone with him.) "Did you set your alarm clock wrong?"

Ryan would smile slyly, but he never had much of an answer. Yet, he began to show up every day some ten minutes early, so I would talk to him, question him, and try to make him laugh. Other early risers in the class also began to talk to him. It seemed that he was making friends outside the few kindred souls he already knew when the class began. However, it was the last day of class when he truly revealed that my loving ways were affecting him.

As I said, on that last day students casually show up to receive their research papers. Some stay for a few minutes, others a bit longer. We speak of future plans and say our good-byes. However, on this sunny spring morning Ryan took the record — staying some ninety minutes. He showed up ten minutes early, as had become his habit. Then he stayed for the entire hour while I passed back papers and alternated between chatting with him and chatting with others as they came and went. When all 23 papers had been handed out and 22 students were gone, Ryan stayed yet another twenty minutes. It was only after I announced that I had to get going did Ryan make his way to leave.

What does this say? What does it mean when a young, seemingly aloof and disinterested eighteen-year-old hangs out with his middle-aged teacher for ninety minutes when a sunny spring day is beckoning? To me it says that Ryan did need what I had to offer: kindness, praise, interest — love. Love in the classroom is not only possible, it is necessary as the key ingredient for miraculous changes in students' lives. I may not ever know what happens to Ryan. I surely believe that my love, the love God makes possible, has touched him in some important way. And I don't feel like I'm done with Ryan yet. Right now, I'm looking for prizes, wondering what a smart-aleck eighteen-year-old would like in his long overdue Easter basket.

Ryan didn't write me a letter at the end of the semester as I asked the students to do. It wasn't his style. The following message I received from another student speaks to the impact of classroom love. This special young lady had revealed to me earlier in the semester that she was gay. Read her response as it appeared on a small green card surrounded by daisies.

- Wendy, I have enjoyed all my classes with you immensely! You're a wonderful teacher and an even more incredible person. Coming into your class I was worried upon finding out you were a Christian. I was afraid you were going to be cruel and judge me. Thank you so much for making those fears disappear. You are a real example of a Christian. You were kind and loving and didn't judge me! Thank

137

you so much; that meant more than I can ever explain. You have given me courage to be proud of who I am! I'm so thankful that I was blessed with the opportunity to have you teach me. Your incredible teaching style will continue to touch lives ... You're an incredible person who shines in the Lord. Keep shining!

From my students' letters and my personal experiences, it seems so obvious that miracles take root and blossom in an environment that shines with God's love. The apostle Paul explained what qualities comprise love, the greatest of all human forces: patience, kindness, generosity, humility, courtesy, unselfishness, good temper, guilelessness, and sincerity. As teachers, we are expected to exemplify these qualities. Mother Teresa told us that, "At the moment of death we will not be judged according to the number of good deeds we have done or by the diplomas we have received in our lifetime. We will be judged according to the love we have put into our work."

Yes, we may excel at creating edge-of-the-seat lesson plans. Yes, our students may reach important objectives prescribed by a course syllabus or state mandate. These are all important goals, worthy plans. But our priority should be putting God's will first. Ask him for miracles! Reach for them! The Bible directs us to a higher purpose: "The human mind may devise many plans, but it is the purpose of the Lord that will be established" (Proverbs 19:21). What is the Lord's purpose for us? The Bible is clear:

> *If I speak in the tongues of mortals and of angels, but do not have love, I am a noisy gong or a clanging cymbal. And if I have prophetic powers, and understand all mysteries and all knowledge, and if I have all faith, so as to remove mountains, but do not have love, I am nothing. If I give away all my possessions, and if I hand over my body so that I may boast, but do not have love, I gain nothing.* — 1 Corinthians 13:1-3

We are told there are three things that last forever: faith, hope, and love. But the greatest of them all is love.

Please take to heart these lessons on teaching with love. Go forth and love your students; love them as God loves you. The students are our work! Labor on your love for them. Care more about them than your culture requires. Transform yourself — your beliefs and your behaviors — and become the miracle you long to see in your students' lives. Gandhi challenged us to be the change we want to see in the world. Take up the challenge and take it with confidence. In the gospel of John, Jesus promises us "... the one who believes in me will also do greater works than these ..." (John 14:12). "Nothing will be impossible for you" (Matthew 17:20b).

Let God's Holy Spirit breathe new life into you, and then let that love uplift you and uplift your students! Hurry! Classroom miracles await!

Appendix:

Proof Of God's
Classroom Power!

Students' Last-Day-Of-Class Letters To The Author

I will greet this day with love in my heart. For this is the greatest secret of success in all ventures ... only the unseen power of love can open the hearts of man. And until I master this act I will remain no more than a peddler in the marketplace. — Og Mandino

As I explain earlier in *Teach And Reach For Classroom Miracles!* I have students write me letters on the first and last day of class. I ask them to be honest and express what they like about the course, what I could do differently to improve it, and to write any other thoughts or feelings they would like to share. There are responses about less work, a better organized course pack, and the like. However, the majority of my students' responses are similar to what you'll read in the next pages. They focus on something much more profound.

I admit that including these letter excerpts does make me a bit uneasy because they express so much praise. It feels very self-congratulatory. I believe that what my students are truly praising is God's love, his Holy Spirit, that is present in my classroom. When we teachers, as imperfect as we are, first strive to teach with God's love in our hearts, that is, with patience, kindness, generosity, humility, courtesy, unselfishness, good humor, honesty, and sincerity, then miraculous thoughts and feelings are what we can expect!

Letters

- I can't thank you enough for helping me realize my potential for writing! You made my start in college easy and fun. I will always remember your kindness!

- I absolutely loved your class. You are one of the best, most encouraging English teachers that I have ever had. I always felt comfortable exploring my style, and I found myself constantly trying to improve my work ... I'm going to miss this class.

- There aren't many teachers that you come by in your lifetime that actually have the ability to help you obtain your goals. You are the first that has shown interest and support in my writing abilities; for that I thank you. I will miss your bright personality every day in class. You have made it fun to come to class, and along the way I have learned quite a bit ... I can only hope you won't forget me, because I know I'll never forget you. Love ...

- I can remember how intimidated I felt the first day of Research. Everyone had told me so many horror stories. However, when you came in the room with your smile and good spirit, you took all my fears away. Thank you for being so motivational; you really helped me gain confidence to do my best. I wish you the best of luck teaching. Your great personality will win the hearts of many.

- Thank you so much for being such a great teacher. More importantly, thank you for being the person you are. I enjoyed having you teach me, especially because of your joy-filled personality. I loved walking into a 9 a.m. class to see you excited and pumped up for the day ... I love the way you teach. This class was very personal. I think you brought out a lot in each student ... You're a very understanding and genuine person. Thank you for all that you taught me. God bless.

- ... how I feel about you and your class. I loved it! I feel like I learned more in this semester in your class than I did my whole high school English career. I love all the assignments of the semester, and I enjoyed your teaching styles and your good humor ... I loved what you got to do and share and experience and what we experienced from you. You always seemed to be having a good time ... I think it was an excellent experience and an excellent start to my college career.

- I couldn't have hoped for a cooler English teacher than you. You have helped me a lot with understanding writing and discovering different techniques. I've learned so much over the last two classes with you. Collectively, I think your class is great ... I find that I have more confidence in my writing than before. You're a wonderful, fun, and energetic teacher that is awesome at your job, and I know that you can get across to your students in your own way ... I am sad to no longer be part of the class. I hope the best for you in the future. May your life be fun and interesting for all time. Don't forget the beat is what makes the world go round, and music can heal. Feed your dog right and stay healthy. Don't ever forget (us) because we will always be friends with you ... *Carpe Diem/Carpe Nocturnum.*

- I cannot begin to describe what a pleasure it was for me to have been a student of yours this past semester. I found the class to be stimulating, as well as challenging ... once I became involved in the projects, it seemed as though my mind, as well as the world, was opening up with every word I wrote. I appreciated the freedom that you allowed me to fully express my thoughts ... I have to say that entering the classroom was a completely different experience; no procrastination or lack of enthusiasm there. I always knew that you would have something thought-provoking and intellectually invigorating to talk about. I was honored to be a part of it ... I want to thank you for the short but deep conversations that we shared in the off moments. They touched me, and I always departed with something to think about ... I was blessed to have met you.

145

- This was my first semester of college ... I was entered into a new and different world known as college. I was afraid that I would only be known as a number, but in your class I was on a first-name basis ... walking in to see a friendly face, a warm smile, and a handshake.

- ... you helped me in multiple ways. You are the type of instructor that is rarely experienced. You help beyond your limit and you motivate the class with your personality ... you have helped me in so many ways with English and real-life matters.

- You helped to make my writing blossom ... I enjoyed your class every day; there was never a dull moment. I made new friends there, and I became a much better writer.

- I really thought you did great at teaching the class. College is a stressful time, and you made the class enjoyable. I liked that you tried to get to know your students, giving us encouraging feedback all throughout your class ... Overall, thank you for a great semester; I had fun.

- You were always willing to give advice and lend a hand when you could. I also very much appreciate your big heart and understanding.

- You made me realize critical thinking is everything.

- It's been a pleasure. I know I haven't been the easiest student to have. I appreciate all the time you've taken with me. All the talks we've had have helped me a ton.

- I really liked how you were one-on-one with every student. I can't speak for the rest of the class, but I greatly appreciated how much you helped me ... I'm glad that I had a teacher like you that I could talk to about whatever I wanted, class-related or personal ... I know it really made a difference to get an English instructor with a positive attitude.

- I thought this class was perfect. I thought that it was challenging at times, and other times it was fun.

- It is very evident ... you really care about all your students ... You definitely made the class fun and encouraged us to participate and for us to make it fun for the whole class.

- I'm so glad I had someone like you as an English instructor.

- I wouldn't change anything about this class. It was great.

- I am sad to see this semester end. I have truly enjoyed you as my English teacher ... Many teachers say they will meet you halfway, and they don't, but you said it and were willing, too.

- It has been an absolute pleasure having you as both my English 101 and 102 teacher. English has always been an enjoyable subject to me, but you brought that to a whole new level. Your encouragement and motivation made me feel that much more confidant about expressing my opinion and my writing in general. I also would like to express my gratitude for being as patient and sympathetic as you were when I would miss an assignment or due date. Many teachers do not show their students the respect that you do. You truly are here to help us, and you have no idea what that means to me. Your words always made me feel really good about my writing, so I hope my words make you feel really good about your teaching!

- You are an excellent teacher and have provided me with such helpful instructions. God has truly graced you with a gift for teaching! I have learned many skills in your class that will help me through the rest of college. I pray that God will continue to bless you and watch over you and all that you do! May our lady and his holy angels protect you!

*And may the Lord make you increase
and abound in love for one another and
for all....*
— 1 Thessalonians 3:12

Printed in the United States
151823LV00002B/5/P